STREB

HOW TO BECOME AN
EXTREME ACTION
HERO

ELIZABETH STREB

FOREWORD BY ANNA DEAVERE SMITH
& INTRODUCTION BY PEGGY PHELAN

THE FEMINIST PRESS
AT THE CITY UNIVERSITY OF NEW YORK
NEW YORK CITY

Published in 2010 by the Feminist Press
at the City University of New York
The Graduate Center
365 Fifth Avenue, Suite 5406
New York, NY 10016
feministpress.org

This book was supported by a Face Out grant
funded by The New York Community Trust,
and administered by the Council of Literary
Magazines and Presses.

THE NEW YORK
COMMUNITY TRUST

First printing April 2010

Cover design by Aaron Henderson, aaronhenderson.com
Book design by Drew Stevens

Library of Congress Cataloging-in-Publication Data

Streb, Elizabeth.
 Streb : how to become an extreme action hero / by Elizabeth Streb.
    p. cm.
 ISBN 978-1-55861-656-1
1. Movement, Psychology of. 2. Human beings—Attitude and
movement. 3. Dance. I. Title.
 BF295.S87 2010
 792.8092--dc22

                                                    2009052614

STREB HOW TO BECOME AN EXTREME ACTION HERO

for

CAROLYN ELLIOT GALE

CONTENTS

Foreword by Anna Deavere Smith   Ix

Introduction by Peggy Phelan   xvii

IN THE BEGINNING   2

Real Estate   11

Birth of STREB   17

A Real Move   21

Music   26

BODY   30

Danger   39

PopAction   41

Extreme Action Specialist   45

SPACE   52

Arena   59

Un-Habitual Space   63

Perspective   65

Perception of Movement   70

Action Machines   81

TIME 96

Hunks of Action 99
How Soon is Now? 103
Real Time 105
Rhythm 113
The Ten-Second Dance 115
Invisible Forces 120

MOTION 126

Fight or Flight 132
Syntax of Movement 136
The Moveical 141

THE REAL MOVE 148

Notes 154
Appendix A: Action Heroes
by Laura Flanders 157
Appendix B: Q&A
Anna Deavere Smith and Elizabeth Streb 164
Acknowledgments 183
Index 188

FOREWORD

Anna Deavere Smith

Elizabeth Streb is a rascal, a brilliant rascal. I enjoy her. What I enjoy the most is the fun. She'd probably prefer that I praise her thirsty, fearless flirtation with disaster, the dazzling originality of her work, or her magnificent mind. Her mind constantly surprises me. It reminds me of one of Louise Nevelson's works. But in addition to that, I like the fun. Streb would find this impossibly sentimental. "Fun?" But the fact is, if you go to a Streb matinee, you will find a throng of kids, completely enthralled, having fun.

The first time I saw Streb, she projected seriousness. It was in a post-show interview following a performance at The Joyce, where a dancer jumped through sugar glass. I was given goggles upon entering the theater, because my seat was in the front row. I was shocked by everything I saw. Streb seemed impatient, even humorless, as she begrudgingly answered questions. Having now had the opportunity to see her in a variety of contexts—at a pre-show in her own S.L.A.M. lab, revving up a crowd of six- to twelve-year-olds, at a dinner I put together with physicists and artists at NYU, and in a number of other social situations—I think she was performing. I bet post-performance discussions tickle her. The word "tickle" will make her gag. I bet she looks forward to these interviews, thinking hard the night before about what to wear. At this interview, she had not yet cut her hair into a mohawk. As I recall, she had a matter-of-fact bob. I believe she was wearing black pants and a French fisherman's sweater.

The next time I saw Streb was six years later at the sixtieth birthday party of the first-ever supermodel, Lauren Hutton. I was sitting alone, watching the parade of legendary models in spike heels and all manner of clothing, and thinking about how these women had spent a substantial part of their lives learning and practicing how to get people to look at their bodies, and how to grab the attention of any passerby, in real time, or on a magazine rack.

I didn't recognize the irony at the time, but as I watched the parade, I was about to meet Streb, the person who would teach me the virtues of looking beyond the body's beauty to the action it creates or responds to. Streb and her girlfriend, Laura, sort of sneaked up beside me, grinning and claiming to be fans of mine. By then, Streb had cut and sculpted her hair into a mohawk and was wearing a very wild-looking man's suit, with a huge medallion around her neck, perhaps a peace sign. Her girlfriend, a pretty blond with an English accent, was dressed in a kind of combination of downtown hip with a tad of preppiness, just a tad (left over from her Barnard days, I suppose). I don't think Streb and Laura were really fans. I now know that Brice Marden's wife, Helen Marden, one of the hosts, and a member of Streb's board, had instructed them to come over and talk to me. In what could not have amounted to much more than three minutes, I noticed some mischief in Streb. Her smile is a unique combination of sizing you up, figuring out what prank to pull on you, and seeing immediately the best in you, the way your fantastic grandmother (the only person who values the real you) would. I wondered what she'd find interesting in a room of iconic models. After all, the only work of hers I had in my mind was one where a woman jumped through glass. The objectives of the super-models surrounding us were preservation of the body and using the body to grab attention. Streb does not want us to look at her dancers' bodies beyond the action they are doing.

Models spend a lot of time in front of mirrors. Streb hates mirrors. She managed to learn to be a dancer without looking in one; she says she crossed her eyes as she faced the mirror. Yet, to become an iconic beauty for hire, one must ultimately be a rascal and a ruthless one. One must break barriers, scorch earth, take over territory, or find a place that is yet unoccupied. Case in point, Iman was in that gathering.

Those representatives of physical beauty, who perpetu-ate all the myths, endure psychic and physical pain if need be—in this way, the legendary models in that room were as outrageous as Streb. Spike heels, mohawks, motorcycle boots, mini skirts, women with thirty-six-inch inseams: it's all extravagant. Tricks, in the end. You must have a sense of humor about your power to grab attention, and a deep un-derstanding about why humans watch, and what they are looking for. Lauren was on more than twenty *Vogue* covers, and yet, I don't think of her as a victim of any gaze. She'd look in the camera and pretend she was on safari, looking out at the wild. Streb doesn't want audiences to look at the bodies of her dancers but she chooses pretty people to be in her company. She understands why people are watching and then takes them deeper. Like those prancing, laughing, smoking, dancing models, Streb seems to me to be a creature, a magnificent, fascinating *creature* with many layers.

A few years later I went to interview Streb at her S.L.A.M. studio for my play, *Let Me Down Easy*, about the human body. The idea was that I would perform Streb among a variety of other real people. The minute I walked into her world, I fell into amazement and awe with the phenomenon of Streb and all things of "Strebness." The room reminded me of the circus. People were falling from thirty feet. There seemed to be a million things going on, and Streb was hunched over a small table, similar to an old-fashioned school desk, in the midst of it. She looked small in stature because the lab is so huge, the machinery so massive, the colors so primary and strong. People were literally bouncing off of walls, falling backwards upon command, screaming out to each other as they ran under, around, and on top of threatening looking wheels, rails, and levers. I was offered coffee. It arrived in a paper cup. Streb seemed appalled that I was being handed a paper cup and told the bearer to put it into a real cup. I insisted that the paper cup was fine, but made a note. It seemed curious that she'd be concerned about what kind of cup her guest had.

I had planned to spend one hour, but was there for at least two. I returned the next day, still mesmerized. Dancers were in front of us dodging a huge metal bar that moved in a circle. I kept shouting out involuntarily, "Watch out!" or "Oh my God!" Everyone was amused. I couldn't stop myself. "Oh my God!" was my descant that day, as I sat at one edge of Streb's small desk, sipping coffee, and talking to her about her work. When I look back on it, I marvel at how Streb was able to have a very concentrated conversation and still not miss a beat on the multiple things going on in her space. I never felt that she was distracted. *I* was distracted. There was just so much for me to *look* at. Most of my interview experiences are about what I *hear*. Although I had probably about two hundred interviews at that point, I knew immediately that I would put her in my show because of the following conversation. She was talking about a fire dance that she had made for her girlfriend's fortieth birthday. And right after she began the dance, for a room of about one hundred people, she accidentally caught on fire:

> And I'd rehearsed it [so, I mean completely] and uh, and I flew . . . you fly . . . you go into a crouch. And then at this certain moment you fly into a flying, horizontal X. And land. Oh, I made the fire as big as this torso part. So I would *smoosh* it. But big enough so you see the fire, but not so big that it went outside my body cuz I would just *smoosh* the oxygen out of it.
>
> I *landed* on it. But unbeknownst to me, I'd been rehearsing, an' I had some Sterno, on my torso? So when I went like *ooom!* like that, and I looked under, an' I go, Oh, uh-oh, I'm on fire. An' *uuh!* I *smoosh* it, an' I, Oh that's not gonna happen. So I stood up an' I was literally on fire. An'. . . I mean I was just like . . . then I went like this? . . .

an' it was the fastest phenomenon ever seen. I've *never* seen anything move that fast. Be that fast. An' you knew, I was like "kay."

She had successfully put action into words, with all those sounds—"oom!" "uuh!" even "uh-oh." As a student of theater, I am looking for words as action, action *in* words—not words *about* action. The interview turned out to be an important part of my show. The show had four different versions before it made it's way to New York. Although many characters hit the cutting room floor somewhere in the journey, my portrayal of Streb was in every one. The audience talks back to her, gasps at her, laughs at her—just as the rambunctious and excited audiences who see her work do.

I exchanged some e-mails with Streb the spring, summer, and fall that followed that interview. In one of them I told her that I was interested in the relationship between understanding and action. She told me that she is all about actions that leave you trying to understand *what just happened.*

I now meet with Streb whenever we are both in town, which is not as often as I would like, but it's part of my ritual, sending a text or an e-mail. "Where are you?" The "where" she is could be Kenya, the Caribbean, Europe.

Streb likes nice restaurants. But if I asked her to show me how to fall backwards in the middle of one of them, she would. She is made of steel, I think. I had a small dinner party and included among the guests were Streb, a former world champion heavyweight boxer, a rodeo bull rider, a model, and a dancer. During cocktails, Streb immediately gravitated toward the heavyweight boxer. I have a film of her sidling up to him (and he is a mansion of a man), looking him up and down, and asking him, "Uhh, how do you take the hit?"

What keeps me listening to and looking at Streb is the well of joy she carries, and the warmth of her heart. She'll hate reading that part. Streb likes fine red wine. When we meet it's usually over a bottle of red wine and there never seems to be enough time. Time *flies*. Streb would say that there is only *now*. And that's how I feel in her presence. There is only now. In something as simple as meeting for a cup of coffee, I get sucked into her now, and end up inevitably screaming, "Oh my God, look what time it is!" I go running off like a character from *Alice in Wonderland*, usually to Streb's amusement. Since she is always in the now, she's never rushing, and she's rarely late. This must be due to the quality of her concentration and her ability to bring a magnified presence to any situation. Commanding. No doubt, she sees more seconds than most of us do in any given half-minute. So in preparation for introducing this book, I asked her to meet me backstage between shows on a two-show Saturday. I put down a bottle of nice red wine on the dressing room table, and put a clock in front of us (see page 164). The interview would last, I said, half an hour, thirty minutes, not thirty-one, not thirty and ten seconds. Whatever got said would be it. Limits seemed appropriate, since Streb works within graceless limits, like gravity. She is constantly breaking through boundaries in spite of the limits. On a daily basis, she is looking for boundaries to cross, walls to break through. I imagine that while most of us look for what's possible, she looks for what's impossible, and offers her hand out . . . for an arm-wrestling match.

New York City
December 2009

INTRODUCTION

Peggy Phelan

Elizabeth Streb's art evokes the dream of flight and the poetry of velocity. Not entirely at home in the vocabularies (or venues) of contemporary dance, Streb prefers to call her art "PopAction." I like that term, although its associative link to cartoons and action heroes risks obscuring the fierce critique of modern dance (and its still persistent attachment to ballet) at the heart of Streb's work. "We don't plié—we fly, explode, and gush into the air." Not for the fainthearted, Streb's work burns with violent beauty.

What most compels me about Streb's work is her insistence that the body is unthinkable without a fully launched understanding of motion: there is no living body at rest—cells, blood, and oxygen move through it even when one lacks consciousness. Thus to be embodied is to be in a state of action. Dance and other disciplines dedicated to movement (from track and field to particle physics) offer us various ways of responding to a body moving toward or away from something other than itself—a cell, a wheel, a wave, a grip, a wrist, a palm, a knee, a hand, a heart.

In my years as a spectator of Streb's performances in New York and more recently as an interlocutor with her at Stanford, I have found myself cobbling together a vocabulary for her work with roots in comic books such as *Batman* and *Popeye*—"Bam!" "Pop!" "Pow!"—and with insights indebted to trauma, religion, engineering, and visual studies. The combination of Streb's dogged pursuit of the physics of the crash and her childlike desire to escape gravity and fly gives her work a sometimes contradictory character—it is at once punishing and beautiful. Insofar as Streb's work is choreography, the body-writing she pursues is propulsive and surprising. The local grammar of the individual dancing body finds its place in the larger syntax of embodied motion. This traversal from the specific to the general recalls the theory (and prose style) of Edmund Burke, the eighteenth century philosopher, who also tried to write about the beauty in the muscle of motion. He called this beauty grace:

> Gracefulness is an idea belonging to posture and motion. In both these, to be graceful, it is requisite that there be no appearance of difficulty; there is required a small inflection of the body; and a composure of the parts in such a manner, as not to encumber each other, not to appear divided by sharp and sudden angles. . . . But as perfectly beautiful bodies are not composed of angular parts, so their parts never continue long in the same right line. They vary their direction every moment, and they change under the eye by a deviation continually carrying on, but for whose beginning or end you will find it difficult to ascertain a point.*

*Burke, Edmund. "Grace," Part III, Section XXII of *A Philosophical Enquiry into the Origins of Our Ideas of the Sublime and Beautiful*, 1757.

Thinking about Burke, I sent Streb an e-mail asking: "Is 'grace' a word you use in relation to your choreography?" She replied the next day:

> I do have an opinion on the idea of Grace, as it relates to Motion—as opposed to sound or painting or literature—[it] has to do with issues concerning transitions. Which requires a decision—when does a moment shift to the next moment? If quintessentially Grace was tantamount to "no transitions"—then how? Could I/we/they decide when the absolution of the "seam" or the "transition" had finally occurred (I will address this idea more-) later . . .

Streb's reply fascinated me both substantively and grammatically. Grace is "tantamount to 'no transitions.'" But what then to make of the transitions at work in Streb's definition? Caps, dashes, questions marks, inverted commas, sentences, and phrases whose precise beginning and ending are hard to discern tumble across the screen. E-mail is often written hurriedly and is closer to the breath than more polished prose. Her blunt certainty about the definition of grace in relation to the quite dizzying depth of the questions that followed keyed me into the nature of her habit of mind. To move from the ground of a definition marked as "tantamount" to the non-ground of time, phrase, division, and grammar itself (parens and hyphens and oddly placed question marks and slash marks and the spit-and-a-promise of the final clause leading to "later," the spill of the words themselves) was to experience a rhythmic darting between large abstraction and the specific demands of the local phrase.

I was struck too by the density of the phrase the "absolution of the seam." No less than mystics and devotees, artists often believe in absolution, a release from the discipline demanded by their art. What exactly absolves one from the need to bow to transitions? Is there such a thing as endless flow? Might it be captured by prose, or does that (imagined) capture halt such ideal flow? Might it be approached through tireless motion, by a body spinning in a wheel, flying toward a wall? When does an upward leap obviate the gravity of the certain fall? And when, oh when, will the promised "later" arrive? This oft-invoked "later" acts as plea or prayer in which we promise to explain ourselves with complete clarity, perfect phrases, transparently clear idiom, some other (always deferred) time—that time of grace in which transitions across seam's time (past, present, future) are not needed. That time of grace when later is now and now is not yet then. "Presentness is grace," wrote Michael Fried long ago and far away in a sentence that floats into the melody of my memory without transition from me to him.

For Streb, erasing the seam, blurring the phrase, is part and parcel of creating fluid motion. At first this may seem counterintuitive in regard to a choreographer whose every phrase seems preoccupied with thwarting flow and motion. In one of her pieces, dancers bang against a clear Plexiglas wall, miked for impact: *Thwack. Boom. Thud.* Streb's dancers "play" the wall, and make it shudder and vibrate as they slam into it, creating a score for trauma. As their increasingly sweaty bodies leave more and more visual traces on the once clear wall, the lines demarcating the moment of arrival and the moment of departure become smeared, blurred, impossible to discern. As these lines accumulate, they resemble nothing so much as a vertical Jackson Pollock canvas, dripping and oozing lines whose density resists all plotting. The glass wall absorbs more than the physical gravity of the dancers' bodies accelerating force; the glass creates an end-stop, a punctuation mark more menacing than the exclamation point. For it says simultaneously "stop at once" and "don't ever stop." This paradoxical contradictory performance renders the usual habit of noting movement phrases, and easeful or awkward transitions in dance, pointless. Indeed, to be *en pointe* in Streb's choreography is to be, quite peculiarly, precisely, and oxymoronically, without ground.

This too is the position Streb offers readers of this book, which is at once memoir, polemic, scholarly investigation, psychoanalytic testimony, love story, and documentary history. A beauty that refuses to hold still long enough to be taken in, a girl who won't settle nicely into the nomenclature of woman, an artist who not so secretly wants to be a scientist, a voice looking for her mother tongue, a hand hooking a fish, a back rattled by a cross-country motorcycle trip—the stories that create and erase the seams in this book are knotted and gnarly rather than smooth and elegant. The writer-scholar in me wants to translate it for younger choreographers just starting out and therefore eager for brashness, which is often misunderstood as sensational pop, rather than rigorous focus. The writer-artist in me wants merely to plead that the aspiration to investigate the nature of time and space within and across a moving body, rather than accepting their measure without question, yields something profound about bodies and time/space. The violence of that encounter can be off-putting but if one can find the capacity to dwell in the trauma, rather than rush to cure it, a terrible beauty may emerge.

To live and write and move with the aspiration to erase the seams is extraordinary, exhilarating, and daunting at once. It is tempting to speculate psychoanalytically about Streb's adoption, her lifelong attraction to Flanders as home (her childhood home was in a town called Flanders, her partner's name is Laura Flanders), her pursuit of the *enfant terrible* role well into her upper-middle age. And had I world enough and time, I would indulge that temptation. But I do not so let me simply say that Streb has been, literally, on fire because of the ideas in this book. The fire was a "failed" birthday gift to Laura, a gift that no doubt caused scars and seams. But the smoking gift also allies Streb with Joan of Arc, brilliantly evoked by Antonin Artaud at the end of his *Theatre and Its Double*: "If there is still one hellish, truly accursed thing in our time, it is our artistic dallying with forms, instead of being like victims burnt at the stake, signaling through the flames." Streb is no victim; her passion burns and turns the pages here. A lifetime of work, of love, of heroic attempts and rueful mistakes, of challenging thought and brilliant invention created the muscle of this book. Mind it.

Stanford, CA
January 2010

IN THE
BEGINNING

**I can't understand why people are frightened
of new ideas. I'm frightened of the old ones!**
—JOHN CAGE

My adventure in life began with action, and I know it will end with action.

At a young age I began to construct public moments for myself without asking for an audience. I thought I could garner the attention of passersby and loiterers, who might be tempted to watch if I paid attention to what was truly unusual. One morning up at Lake Ontario, where my adoptive family had a cottage in a local marina called Flanders, I saw a gaggle of men hovering over something and gesturing wildly. I was eight or so, by which time I was a trained fisherman. I pushed through the crowd and peered down. I saw a four-foot-long eel squirming all over the place in the horrible way snakes, their cousins, can. I saw that it had swallowed a hook. In fishermen's parlance this is a drag because it means you lost your hook and are often forced to re-rig your entire pole.

Once I had forced myself into the center of the men, I bent down, took the eel in my left hand very close to its neck (if eels had necks, which they don't; they are actually *all* neck), got close to the back of its jaw hinge, and squeezed.

ES and Jan Jeffers, her partner in crime, with their day's catch, including an eel. Lake Ontario, 1960.

It opened its mouth and I stuck my entire hand, fingers first, down its gullet, searching around for the hook's hard stem. I got my forefinger just inside the curve of the hook and pushed down hard. The hook got unhinged from the stomach of the eel and out it came. I threw the eel back down to the ground dramatically and handed the hook to one of the men. They screamed and cheered, and said, "That little boy got the hook out! Good fella!" I turned on my heel and walked away, glowing and glowing, hugely proud for hours after. I knew I would tell this story many times over in my future, but I also knew it was an experience that you had to be there for. I could never properly describe in words an event like that.

Another early physically intense memory was putting up a ceiling at our house on the lake. Leonard Streb, my adoptive father, built both our houses by himself, from stuff left over from various jobs (which has always reminded me of Johnny Cash's lyric, "I'd get it one piece at a time / And it wouldn't cost me a dime . . ."). One time, Leonard ran out of nails and asked me to stand on a ladder and hold up a part of the ceiling while he ran to get more materials. My hands were over my head in a parallel fifth position with the heels of my hands flexed hard against the Sheetrock. Minutes passed, but still no sound of his return. I remember thinking, what an asshole. He's at some bar having a beer, thinking this is funny. If I had moved, the pieces he had put up would collapse. I was not going to let that happen.

Before long, my arms started shaking, my shoulders quivering. I started breathing heavily. I tried to name the sensations. I sensed the moments passing: it was authentic slow motion (another idea encased in the term adagio I grew to loathe in dance). I realized back then that there was no vocabulary for fire-in-the-sinews or rapid-quaking-of-muscle-groups. I was experimenting with the application of force, what little I could exert upwards toward the surface I was holding, given my weight and height and generally small size. For some reason, I kept pushing up with new intensity. I would start to feel myself fail, then—*Eureka!*—there'd be a little bit more of me, way down inside. A few hours later he came back and was shocked to find me still there, not because he was impressed, but because he had forgotten all about the ceiling and me.

One time I burnt a big barn down to the ground. I didn't mean to; I was playing with matches in the hay and it caught on fire. It was so magnificent I didn't try to stop it. No one was hurt but it was quite a spectacle. I got a huge amount of attention that day; cars parked everywhere and

Due to ES's early pyromanaical tendencies, her father and Uncle Elmer's barn goes up in flames, 1961.

people stood around to watch. I was interviewed by the police, who threatened to take me to juvenile court. I admitted it was my fault. I knew I shouldn't lie, but I also knew I shouldn't talk about the small, amazing pockets of fire, how their power excited me: something so tiny could wreak such havoc.

In 1968, after years of performing unspecific action in the world, I looked at the list of possible majors at the State University of New York in Brockport, New York, and chose dance. This seemed to be the perfect combo of art and movement. Rose Strasser, the chair of the dance department, interviewed me and noticed I had no dance credentials.

"What can you do?"

"Well, I can pick up any disco dance that comes along.

I get the rhythm instantly and can teach it to all my high school girlfriends! Does that count?"

"No," she said, "That has nothing whatsoever to do with dance."

Twenty years later I came to realize that that might be exactly what is wrong with modern dance.

Four years after that moment, I got onto my Honda 350 and tore out of Rochester, New York, *Easy Rider*-style, with exactly $120 cash, which I earned from training as a mechanic in a gas station and pumping gas. I headed west to San Francisco, arriving there a mere thirty days and six thousand miles later, via New Orleans, Houston, Colorado

ES with her Honda 350, 1972. Photo: Kate Robertson Fisher.

Springs, and Albuquerque, with a few other stops along the way. To date, this was the most grueling physical act I ever performed. I am still vibrating from that journey.

In time, I knew my life had to be built in New York.

I moved to New York City in 1974 and got my first job at the Wild Mushroom Café on Bleecker Street. There I met a guy named James. I was introduced to him by another new friend, Jimmy Gambino. Jimmy was once a Golden Gloves champion, but had gotten into a bad drug habit and lost his legs. He walked with two canes and made a rhythmic sound as he came down the street. Part of the sound was his two artificial legs, not just the canes. I was scared of him, scared of that impending sound and what it signified. One time I found a booklet of American Express checks. I asked Jimmy to cash them in for me. I knew he knew people who could do this. He said, "No, Elizabeth. You don't want to get mixed up in that." I completely thought I did, but I trusted him to know better, and didn't ask twice.

So James was the "block guy" on Bleecker Street. He had access to cheap apartments, from $110 to $225 a month. If you put down a key deposit of a couple hundred dollars, you could get a lease. This was prime property in New York City. It still is. This was an early clue to New York real estate: it mattered who you knew. Those with their hands on the strings of power were not always behind a desk. They often wandered around the streets where you would least expect to find powerful, influential people.

When I first began working at restaurants, I knew I wasn't ready to begin as a cook. Sure, I could read a recipe and make a meal. But could I read it in five seconds, make it in ten, and do it absolutely consistently night after night? Could I take the pressure? I needed training first.

So I started as a porter, which basically meant I got up very early to clean restaurants before they opened for business and before my daily 10 a.m. dance class. At one point, I was whizzing on my bicycle to clean three restaurants in downtown New York first thing in the morning. It was a terrible introduction to the trade. At one restaurant, every white shelf was literally covered in rat footprints every morning. Few things unnerved me, but this did. I was relieved when I felt ready to cook. Before long, I had a shift every night of the week. I was making thirty dollars a night. Still, cooking was about the efficiency, accuracy, and exactness of events. It was about being able to stand the heat, literally and figuratively. In small kitchens such as the ones I worked in, the menu is divided up into various cooking zones: stovetop, oven, broiler, and cold station. I worked all these zones at once. It was not unusual for me to cook 150 dinners by myself in one night.

For some reason I remember one night, after many years in the restaurant business, I was walking to work at Charlie and Kelly's on West Fourth Street. I had tears in my eyes, thinking, oh, oh my dream of being a choreographer may not work out. I may have to work in restaurants forever! I was thirty-five years old already, and I was just being realistic. But then I thought, okay, so what. I can live with that. If that is my fate, aren't I better off than most people in the world? I was feeling sorry for myself, which is why the moment stands out for me. Of course, I didn't have to work in

ES cooking at Charlie and Kelly's restaurant in the West Village, 1977.

restaurants forever, and I've been able to dedicate myself to choreography full-time for many years. And I might as well state the obvious: it's much easier to be successful than to struggle through a horrible job. But that doesn't mean you discover more in your life. The information I got working as a restaurant cook added to my knowledge of movement, and enhanced my lexicon, even if it wasn't being recorded, and even if no one important noticed me.

REAL ESTATE
In 1977, I was breaking up with my first girlfriend, Paige. Well, she was breaking up with me. I was still madly in love with her when she decided to walk out, to go with another woman. Apparently I didn't pay much attention to her. I had rehearsals and two classes a day, I cooked six nights a week, and I was completely unaware of the normal demands of a relationship. I have a memory of sitting in front of the TV eating coffee ice cream, hearing a sound, turning around and Paige was asking me something, wanting something. I thought, can't she see I'm busy? It never occurred to me that being with someone meant sometimes not doing exactly what you felt like. I trouble to mention this break-up for two reasons. One is about relationships, which I'll return to later. The other is about fire escapes. During our break-up, I decided to climb down mine to look into Paige's apartment (we lived on different floors in the same building). I saw exactly what I feared most, and despite all the climbing and jumping I would do in the future, this was the last time I exercised that option at home. And then I needed to move.

I met Tom Treadwell in ballet class around this time. He and I decided to look for a place together. A lot of artists were heading south to find cheaper work/living spaces. I thought that if I could build a studio to rehearse and live in and rent it out to other dancers, maybe I could cut down on my cooking time. Tom found a loft at 307 Canal Street at Broadway. We signed the lease together for three thousand square feet of raw space at $450 a month. Raw space means no electricity, water, plumbing, stove, sink, toilet, interior doors, walls. Raw space! We knew we had to create everything from scratch, but we didn't know about the rats, scores of them. Tom found out on the very first evening, when the sun went down across the horizon of the floor plan. Dozens and dozens of rats walked across the floor towards Tom, who ran to the restaurant where I was working that night to tell me. Rats again!

We learned that rats in New York City are in fact super-rats, impervious to any poison. You could maybe catch them in traps, but rarely would even a powerful spring-release contraption actually kill them. We tried glue traps, which were even worse. When they got caught, they were famous for the most intrepid escapes, like chewing off their appendages, which we would inevitably encounter elsewhere later on. They were fearless eating machines, and never stopped chewing. A friend told me the only way to get rid of rats for good was to shoot them. I imported a gun from a friend in Long Island, where they were legal, and began target practice on the ones stuck in the glue traps.

To build out the loft, Tom and I spent every penny we made. In the summer of 1977, Leonard Streb came down on the Amtrak from Rochester with his toolbox and know-how. He put up every single one of the five hundred two-by-fours and leveled the bathroom floor. He couldn't believe that my handsome roommate wasn't much help: "What the hell is wrong with him? Six feet four inches tall and he can't pound a nail in straight!" But I helped him, as I used to do as a girl. It was the most decent act he ever performed for me.

The place started to look more and more like a gorgeous dance studio, and so it became one. I bought Tom out after eighteen months. He didn't want to live in public anymore; he wanted a home. I deeply did not want a home. I wanted to run a public space, and for many years I lived there as well. I rented out the space by the hour, and never made more than it cost me to live and work there. In 1980, the landlord, Max Landau, took me to court to get the space back. It wasn't legal residential property, so he thought he would kick us out and make money with new tenants who would pay four times as much for the same property. The property value had risen exponentially. He owned Industrial Plastics, the store below my loft, and he sued me and the five other residents of the building who also refused to vacate. He knew we were living there illegally from the start, making a less expensive home than others in the neighborhood at that point. But we not only improved his physical property by investing tens of thousands of dollars in renovations, we improved the entire neighborhood. This was becoming a typical Manhattan feud. When we finally settled the case in court in 1995, our side prevailed. He gave us each another raw space in the building, with a forty-five-year lease and the right to purchase (at a very low price) in time. Tenants like us are now protected under the New York City Loft Law, which passed in 1982.

Throughout this long battle, I remained on civil terms with the landlord. And I learned an important lesson about time and space and relationships when it comes to real estate in New York City.

It was 1995 when I moved out of my three-thousand-square-foot loft and began looking for a different kind of space for my extreme action company, STREB. By now I had developed a practice that involved eight dancers and tons of action equipment. We were rehearsing in several different garages and lofts in Brooklyn, Queens, and on the West Side of Manhattan. Down the street from one of the garages on North Sixth Street in Williamsburg, I saw a phone number that led me to a man in real estate named Carl Vollmer. I called him for months and months, telling him what kind of garage would be STREB's dream space. He would retort, "Don't tell me your hopes and dreams! It'll cost you seven thousand dollars a month and that's that!" After several months of these exchanges on the telephone, he told me to meet him at Bedford and North Seventh Street. We walked to 51 North First Street, to a former loading facility for the Old Dutch Mustard Company. I looked into this vacant space, with thirty-foot-high ceilings and a fifty-by-one-hundred-foot footprint, and I saw the potential for magic everywhere and Carl helped make that happen.

I began the journey to acquire it with a ten-year lease. Then in November 2007, with unprecedented support from the New York City Department of Cultural Affairs, the New

ES in the garage that became S.L.A.M. when it was first delivered to her "broom clean," shortly after signing her ten-year lease, April, 2002.

York City Council, the Mayor's Office, and the Brooklyn Borough President's Office, STREB purchased the space, which had become the STREB Lab for Action Mechanics (S.L.A.M.).

S.L.A.M. is an anti-white cube, anti-glass bubble, anti-ivory tower arena. It's the un-Lincoln Center. It's an experiment of place. It is the urban barn modeled after the suburban garage, which has been the birthplace of astounding new genres: rock 'n' roll, high-tech industries, chemistry experiments, grunge, etc. A place where "wrecking" the place doesn't matter. Unlike theaters or dance studios, a garage *is* a place to eat, drink, destroy, and build. We wanted to strip away the veneer of privilege, and appear as an entity more grounded in the hubbub of real time and daily life.

Over the past seven years we've developed a new operating system for audience sovereignty. Our new rules of conduct for twenty-first century audiences include: no start time; question necessary duration; no exclusion of noise; leave the house lights on; eat, drink, and be merry; do whatever you want, whenever you can; have all ages, races, classes together for a common purpose; mingle economic yields of buildings in adjacent neighborhoods; multitask; have no doors; offer things people need, like bathrooms and water; drop the idea of beginning, middle, and end; forget the idea that events have some pre- intended meaning; know that subjects are dead, it's all verbs; immerse with strangers; question civic duty; find your real audience on your own, virally; make an event a destination for more than one reason; ask what's an accidental "art-act"; be "open source," it's a Wikipedia world; believe Jane Jacobs in the *Death and Life of Great American Cities*; ask what is the next "small thing"; redesign lobby use; question the frozen real estate of fixed seating; question the hidden messages in the theater ticket; notice the difference between a metro ticket, movie ticket, and bus ticket; embrace interruption; examine public vs. private; examine the sidewalk, the low water line, and porches; redesign audience experiences; leave cell phones on; ask what can you sell? who wants what you have? what do you have?; re-examine the issue of scale; question what's right-sidedness; let outside in and inside out; lose ideas of ordained behavior; ask what is a new cultural paradigm; embrace distraction; let your mind wander; let kids, their behavior and desires, lead the way; install popcorn and cotton candy machines; intersect peoples' necessary everyday pathways; speak to a "smelly" person today; put a public sidewalk through your building; install audience action karaoke. Experience is a verb.

BIRTH OF STREB

My dance company STREB began with a dream of flight, rugged and rough, downward-bound, dealing with true space, the sky, an area above the ground. Our aspirations are subject to the problem of how to get up into the air, then manage the land, which is just below the sky's southern edge and what is immutable: the end of space, the hegemony of the bottom, the savagery of the ground. Impact is a primal and primitive practice we at STREB accept: the full, weighted human body, with its issues of vectors and forces

ABOVE: ES in her piece, "Target," 1983. Photo: Lois Greenfield.

OPPOSITE: ES in her piece, "Little Ease," 1999. Photo: Peter Rad.

STREB: In the Beginning

19

and angles of incidence and choices that are incurred in a flash of an instant, yet determine everything. Our spirits rise a half second before the ground-rush intersects with our body, our blood, and our bones.

Everything about STREB Extreme Action concerns the search for what in the world might constitute a real move. We are not trying to invent something that already exists: we are trying to locate, define, and recognize new, invisible, uncontrollable physical phenomena. Defining the real move is our holy grail, and we know that it has properties that may hold certain surprises, certain secrets that might be alarming and dangerous. Our job is to present extreme action events on earth in the artificial places called theaters; we feel a responsibility and an interest in contributing to

LEFT: "Headstand," Muscle Beach, Santa Monica, CA, 1954. Photo: Larry Silver. Courtesy of George Eastman House, International Museum of Photography and Film. RIGHT: "Fly," Coney Island, NY, 1998.

the action lexicon that hasn't yet been built to enrich the language of movement. In linguistics, a lexicon means the complete set of meaningful units in a language. That is what we want our movement lexicon to include. We want to determine which parts of action *are* meaningful, and what determines meaning in movement.

A REAL MOVE

What is a real move? Let's accept that a real move has three most basic, elemental ingredients—time, space, and body— these three combine to become movement and are jiggled into existence by invisible forces. What, then, is the difference between regular movement and a real move? There are a number of ways I believe they can be distinguished: a real move has the power and depth to create a movement *archetype*. These archetypes are made up of motion first, rhythm second, and image third. They exist as powerfully as narrative or aural archetypes do, but they currently go unnoticed. (I believe these archetypes or memories are stored at the cellular level—chemically, muscularly, and maybe even in the marrow of our bones and in the endings of our nerves.) These memories are not necessarily recalled in a linear or narrative manner. They instead whack into us like a bolt of a new sort of recognition. We can't necessarily call them up at will; they have to be excavated, exploded out of us. But I contend that these hidden memories or forgotten sensations are an important aspect of where the content, or meaning, of the movement as a form resides. Along with the true rhythm of action, these memories are

TOP: Harry Houdini in a straight jacket about to be suspended by his ankles from the top of a skyscraper. BOTTOM: "Squirm," 2001. Photo: Tom Caravaglia.

instead physical, temporal, and spatial. They won't sound or look or smell or feel like normal memories or stories; that is not the nature of movement. I don't believe I have ever experienced a story from movement, but I've experienced much more. Movement is a powerful engraver, not a reference maker or a temporal mimicking machine (as in dance done according to music). All of this is to say that events or dances need to be experienced in time. It is difficult to convey to another person the nature of an experience of a real move or an action event. To really *know*, you had to be there in order to have the experience. I can tell you my eel story, but it's not the same as seeing me take the swallowed hook out of its gullet, and it's definitely not the same as actually doing it.

Let me first define my terms. What exactly do I mean by the term "real"? I have thought about using the word "true" or even "pure" instead of real (they are all apt adjectives), but I believe true is a more clouded term than real, and pure gets into difficult Kantian a priori territory. To quote the *Cambridge Dictionary of Philosophy*: "Kant's critique concerns pure reason because Kant believes these determinations about space and time can be made a priori, i.e., such that their justification does not depend on any particular course of experience (pure and a priori are thus usually interchangeable)."[1] While some would argue that human movement is parallel to Kant's idea of experience, I would suggest that it simply is experience.

Something that is real has no referents, no need to assign it with any true or false statements. It simply is. This is the reason why I refer to a "real move" rather than a "pure move" or a "true move." The *Oxford English Dictionary* defines real as "actually existing as a thing or occurring in fact; not imagined or supposed." From the same source, the philosophic definition of real is, "relating to something as it is, not merely as it may be described or distinguished . . . of a substance or a thing, not imitation or artificial, genuine; true or actual." If something is pure, the same source claims, "it is not mixed or adulterated with any other substance or material; without any extraneous and unnecessary elements, free of any contamination." This word pure seems better suited to the quality of a material substance (referring to drinking water, say) or to intentions, not to a phenomenon that is magical, radical, invisible, and embedded in each of our moments (no movement, no life).

If something is true, philosophers concerned with ontological systems of hierarchy have developed deep methodologies to ascertain its "trueness." True, justified belief is the classical definition of knowledge, for example (this was true at least until Gettier came along in the 1960s). But the appropriate question here is not whether a movement is true in the sense that the word is used in relation to language and meaning. True pertains well to language but is not well-suited to the assessment of movement. Suzanne Guerlac asks: "What happens when we try to consider real movement intellectually? We find that our thought is not cut out for the task. Thinking in time, Bergson writes, will always be incommensurable with language, which crushes duration through its very iterative structure. We repeat the same word to name a variety of things at different moments, when, in actuality, nothing ever occurs in exactly the same way twice."[2] Certainly this is true when considering movement.

It is difficult, if not impossible, to grasp the deepest idea of movement through language. For example, when a critic begins her paragraph with, "This is what happened . . ." or "This is what they did," you know she is missing the point. It isn't what the dancer did descriptively, rather it's what happened to her, and how (in what manner) she did what she did that holds the critical factors of meaning in movement. The phenomenological experience of this happening or this series of movements was transferred to the viewers in an automatic fashion. The experience of the audience, or the witnesses, may never correlate with the intention of the choreographer. This experience, by its very nature, is not purely mental or emotional. There is no doubt a missing vocabulary for writing about movement as subject. I once asked a critic to call the moves by their sounds, to make up words to expand the vocabulary of movement, the way film and architecture and music and math have their own terms. Words and sounds such as swook, swack, whiktok, rackedt, thwack, and kaboom that feel and sound like a move. She said that her editor would fire her; I thought, then let it be.

A move is real if it is irreducible, only itself; if it possesses certain fundamental properties that can be classified. Among those possible properties: it does not seek an alternate meaning; it is a verb; it does; it acts. It does not refer to another idea, or a historic time other than right now, the present tense, this moment that will soon be over. Real movement isn't pretending. Real movement doesn't try to tell a story. It doesn't merely indicate. It is not about anything, separate from itself.

Historically, movement in dance has performed one of three tasks: it fits itself to music (in a move-to-note manner), it tries to express emotion as a primary effort, and it attempts to tell a story. These three activities render action artificial. Choreographers have a responsibility to consider what their discipline—movement—can do that is exclusive to the domain of movement as a language unlike any other. Words are very good at telling a story and so people write books with them. Generally, writers don't cut words out of the page and fling them around the room in front of a live audience. They do not try to make their words dance, not literally anyway. Yet we try to make our moves tell a story. Ridiculous. Over time, filmmakers have worked to understand the function of film: what can film do differently from, say, photographs? Filmmakers can speed up and slow down the passage of events or time. Photos alone cannot do this. Film also has the capacity to make images very large or very small, it can tell stories in a non-narrative way, it can go backward in time. Film directors can also control the audience's angle of viewing in infinite ways. True live-time events or theatrical presentations cannot lend themselves to this type of magic.

MUSIC

Music as a field contends with sounds that often come out of invented contraptions like the piano, the horn, and the guitar, just as our STREB action comes out of invented contraptions—the fly machine, the gizmo, vertical walls—but for different ends. Action is not currently treated as its own subject because what movement itself does best has been severely underinvestigated and not noticed. There is not yet a "moveical" form (in the way that there are musicals or dramas). The fields of drama, music, film, literature, and architecture all have deeply investigated forms, each with their very own nomenclature, a nomenclature that movement currently lacks. Movement is treated philosophically and historically as a stepchild to these other disciplines. In the ensuing chapters, I will elucidate why I believe this is true and various ways this problem can be addressed.

When my life partner, Laura Flanders, turned forty a few years ago, I wanted to give her a supreme and symbolic gift. I conceived of a fire dance, a conceptual one. I named it "BlazeAway." It was performed to a Melissa Etheridge song with the lyric, "I'm the only one who'd walk across the fire for you."

A fire was lit as large as the square my hips outlined. The idea was to walk up to the fire along a narrow lane, just long enough so that by the time I got to the blaze it would be quite large. I crouched down and flew into the air, making a very large horizontal X with my body, arms, and legs, and landed dead center on the flame. It was supposed to go out. But when I looked under my stomach and stood up, I realized that I was on fire, fully ablaze. All one hundred guests stared at me; in fact, my best friend Danita continued to take pictures of the event. I looked down and thought I had NEVER seen anything happen so fast. Fire was climbing upwards and burning through my clothes. I

"BlazeAway," 2009.

patted it, but it was not going to be snuffed out. It got bigger and bigger, faster and faster . . . I thought that in about
a half second my hair would torch and I would ruin my girlfriend's birthday party.

My company has a "call and response" system for
when something goes terribly wrong. The entire team has
the responsibility to call out a command to amend the situation. Whoever calls out first, everyone must obey; it is
the only possible fixer to a physical emergency. In this moment, I was on fire, and one of the dancers screamed out,
"Take it off!" We all interpreted this to mean, remove all
my clothes. Very quickly, one of my dancers grabbed the
cuffs of my pants while I jumped high. They pulled hard,
and my pants were off. I ran out of the room throwing my
shirt behind me.

By this time in my life I was a professional choreographer, but in that moment, I was more in touch with my youthful experiments. I knew this was going too far. This came too close to a movement doing me in. Yet it invoked the genesis of my purpose. I didn't want to do things safely, I didn't want to be careful. I wasn't sorry. This could have been an instance after which I might have regretted that impulse. But I didn't. I escaped.

I wasn't hurt much, just a four-inch square burn on my thigh. I remember feeling the burning while I was on fire, and feeling surprised that I, too, was susceptible to being burned, just like everyone else on earth. I realized that I could literally burn to the ground. This moment was an amalgam of everything I had done before, a perfect symbol for the dramatic physical moment I've wanted to achieve.

Walking around New York City the next day, I felt like a hero. I had gone further than taking a hook out of an eel's stomach. I had been on fire. I looked at complete strangers on the street and thought, you don't realize this, but yesterday I was on fire.

How far am I willing to go? What line will I cross to make an extreme action moment? What am I willing to do? Is there anything I would not be willing to do? I realized then that the bigger challenge is to imagine these moves, these moments. Once I envision them, I know I will do them. I would only be limited by my lack of imagination. That would be the only potential threat to my experiments.

BODY

That man seems to be dancing, but in reality
he's just taking a long time to fall down.
—ROGER BABB, *BRAIN CAFÉ*

From 1967 to 1995, I studied the techniques of Humphrey-Weidman, José Limón, Doris Humphrey, Merce Cunningham, Viola Farber (my teacher from 1974–81), Jeff Slayton, and June Finch (my teacher from 1982–91 and in whose company I danced from 1979–81). I worked with Sondra Fraleigh, Mary Edwards, Santo Giglio, Bill Glassman, and Irma Plyshenko. I also studied ballet with Alfredo Corvino, Janet Panetta, Jocelyn Lorenz, Diana Byer, and Margaret Craske. I was suspicious of many of the training techniques in these fields of dance. Dance teachers employed methods I saw as antithetical to the exercise of a body really moving through space in time. This was no fault of these great teachers; they were passing down traditions (and some were creating new ones as well).

I remain indebted to few extremely encouraging dance teachers from my early years in dance. Daniel Nagrin, one of my teachers at SUNY Brockport from 1969–72, was a powerful influence on me in terms of my early exposure to the art of inventing movement. At that point, I already considered myself an artist. The idea of the creative act

**ES in dance class at Margaret Jenkins Dance Studio
in San Francisco, CA, 1972.**

STREB: Body

was not a foreign one. Under his tutelage, I choreographed my very first dance called SHAM in 1969. Margaret Jenkins was my first professional mentor. I danced in Margy's dance company in San Francisco from 1973–74. Margy then introduced me to everyone she knew in New York City. For years, I relied heavily on her belief in me. When Merce Cunningham and John Cage came to my first full evening of choreography at Dance Theater Workshop in 1981, I believe it was Margy who sent them. Susannah Newman, my dance technique teacher at SUNY Brockport, was, to this day, the best, most profound dancer I have ever witnessed. Susannah was the first person to look me in the eyes and say, "Elizabeth, you're a dancer." This one sentence carried me through many uncertain moments in the intervening years.

I was very clear about what happened to my body when I began to move at any point in time. Something transformative would happen. Engaged in moving, I was not conscious in the same way I am when fewer forces are corralling me, i.e., when I am still. This feeling is highly addictive. I saw movement as a way to truly be in the world, and to understand as fully as possible the most important and non-trivial aspects of the earthly experience. In movement, I could experience the easily lost phenomena of time, space, and invisible forces. The experience felt almost chemical. Time slowed way down, space passed as if it had no choice, and its vapor-like quality became structured into shapes that guided my flight and my traveling by force and necessity. By mixing up a body through motion, I felt that I was able to see and feel the critical factors that structure the world. This would be my way to navigate, I decided. I would dedicate my life to moving and to creating action events, extreme action events—real moves.

In my early training, I immediately took issue with the fact that men got to do the most exciting movements in dance classes. Men lifted women, they performed the grand allegro. It wasn't fair. I got into some gnarly arguments with my ballet teachers over particularly annoying balletic traditions, along with their insistence that I wear pink tights and put my hair back so it would not move. The arguments included not just ones about gender but also more intricate issues about the true nature of a human body in motion. I questioned why women go on point. It is difficult to believe they'd go to all that trouble involving special shoes, broken bones, and bloody toes, just to rise up three inches. I realize that the purpose of many of the moves is to affect (or indicate) lightness and being airborne, but those moves also often require men to assist the women in turns and lifts and certain famous adagios. While watching performances of ballet and certain more conventional modern companies, a thought invariably courses through my brain: *put her down!* As a woman I cannot immerse myself in what those physical situations represent—a captive, helpless place. This seventeenth century habit is alive and well and loved by most choreographers. If every action tells a story of its own, I believe the gender behavior within the form of ballet is utterly past tense, a technique that served to humiliate our species. In the class of Margaret Craske, a deeply respected Cecchetti ballet teacher, I observed that she had been calling certain females the wrong name for ten years. She would magically learn any new male ballet dancers' names the very first time they showed up in class. What is that about? I wondered.

The issue of class, which pervades ballet, is offensive to me as well. Even the training smells of elitism. Margaret Craske would bellow from the front of the room, "Stand straight, don't look down, make your face look beautiful and relaxed. Smile." My Native American friend, Eddy Swimmer, was a gorgeous dancer, but he always looked down at what he was *doing*. He was scolded for it. It seems to me that ballet as a form relates to those who have the luxury to maintain a straight spine, namely those who do not work, or ever lift heavy things, and move them from one place to another, ad infinitum.

I wanted to find a way to be true to my own experience of action, and to locate my interest there. My inspiration and curiosity did not lie in the choices and actions I was asked to perform in the classroom, or in the studio. I tried to zero in on my main interest and to articulate an initial unreachable goal that I would spend the next number of years striving to accomplish.

Still, I wanted to fly. I considered flying and its pursuit a reasonable goal. I still do. The failure to investigate or even attempt human flight is at the heart of the artificiality of the dance field. Most dancers don't seem to believe that the human body could (or should) actually get off the ground, so they fly indicationally, mostly by leaping. To reach up and sway the arms, and then leap and arch at the same time, is close enough to flying for them.

Free falling from on high at S.L.A.M., 2009.
Photo: Tom Caravaglia.

They leapt, this is true, but if you leave earth and your base of support is the bottoms of your feet, and you return to earth via the bottoms of your feet again, you haven't changed your orientation in space. So it's not truly flying; flying is more complex than that. Just glance up at the barn swallows and insects to permit yourself to abandon all ideology of a "bottom" or base while you are "up." Even if you are off the ground, if you are still in vertical space, you're cheating a bit.

In ballet terminology, going onto point constitutes being airborne, it ultimately makes ballerinas appear lighter than all others on stage. I find these acts unbelievable and unsatisfying. True or real flight is much more dangerous. It requires contending with gravity and its effect on the weight of the human body. Intuitively, I feel we have to ask questions about flight. What would human flight look like? We have to eliminate the idea of mimicking birds from our consciousness. We will never fly like birds. We don't have hollow bones or zero body fat or wings and feathers, or ancestors who flew and were helped by evolutionary physical alterations. Perhaps if we had started sooner with our belief in human flight, we'd be flying now.

What we can do is launch our bodies off ledges and hurtle towards the ground at the speed of thirty-two feet per second squared! If you think about it that way, access to flight is everywhere. The issues of how to land and where to jump from are the more pressing concerns. The ground aborts our flight and ends it abruptly, but a technique might exist to solve that problem. In any case, the drama of impact is a powerful metaphor, and mostly an avoided one.

When I first tried to fly, I crashed crudely into the ground. After trying it several times in different ways, I got pretty banged up. As rudimentary as this may seem, it was the genesis of my heuristic method of experimentation with the body. It starts with a simple thought experiment: Can a person fly? Then tasks are set up to address the question, and data is collected. The investigation is based on our STREB agreement that we will not make assumptions about outcomes. We agree to *not know.* As a rubric, we develop the types of questions that you forget to ask because they appear so unquestionably true.

What this flying experiment revealed to me was the existence of forces that never got mentioned in dance class. Impact and the human body have a long, intricate, and violent past. But that wasn't my focus as I flew and fell, over and over again. Instead, I thought about how to shape actions around these forces in such a way as to harness the extra seconds they allowed. Traditional dance movement has left out the issue of all these implementers (forces produced from falling, for instance). Modern dance speaks much more generally about these things. I recall my teachers, as we were dancing, calling out, "Breathe. Lift up. Be more graceful. You're off the beat. Relax." Specific forces were rarely named. The distinction between speed, momentum, acceleration, velocity, and rate was never clarified. A certain aversion to pain also played a role. The carefulness that is employed in dance studios is a killer of great ideas. I think all movement specialists need to agree to get at least a little hurt once they venture into a room to invent action. Dancers spend entirely too much time worrying about themselves and their futures. We at STREB think about pain very differently. We don't use the word pain. After a particularly intense physical experience, we refer to it as another interesting, rather foreign sensation. This practice has opened the floodgates of possibility. Tampering with one's reaction to fear does the same thing.

DANGER

At STREB we set up dangerous conditions that push the human animal outside of its daily comfort zone and into physical territories that provoke the fight or flight response. In his fascinating book *Deep Survival,* Laurence Gonzales comments on the mysterious and murky line that separates the quick from the dead. Practitioners of STREB technique cannot afford the "flight" response to a physical situation. Fast-twitch muscle and instantaneous brain responses are critical in dangerous moments, and these decisions have to happen in a split-second; flinching and pausing at these moments courts destruction and death. In STREB work, second-guessing oneself is anathema to survival, both for oneself and one's teammates.

There is a famous story about the Wallenda Family's pyramid walk, on a tightrope forty feet above the ground. One of the performers, who was on the bottom, made a fatal error—a second guess—which ended in tragedy. Reports say that the performer momentarily released his pole, tossing it slightly in an attempt to gain a more secure grip. The pyramid is said to have collapsed silently in slow motion; the bodies hit the dirt-covered floor nearly forty feet below with the sound an elephant makes when it smacks its trunk on the ground. As hardware riggers in the circus say, the first mistake is one too many.

A STREB action specialist in training to do a real move also needs a constitutionally impervious physical body. There can be no inherent weakness in structure, joints, ligaments, tendons, muscles, mind, or heart. You can't be stronger on the bottom of your body (hips and legs) than you are on the top (torso, arms, and gut). If you want to fly and crash, then everything must be tuned to perfect pitch. The "inside" part of the approach to real movement is even trickier. A real mover's spatial, physical, and temporal curiosity has to be insatiable. The dancers of STREB are action engineers or movement methodologists. Their number one question has to be *how*, not *why*. They can never say no. The book *The New American Circus* talks about the training of a circus performer—a trapeze artist: "For flexibility Miguel jumped rope vigorously every single day. Two or three times a week he lifted weights. He didn't want muscles that would be too stiff; they are not fast enough in the air. He did one hundred pushups every a.m. and every p.m., and he and Juan boxed almost every day because it was good for their reflexes and because it got them used to feeling sudden jarring blows on the face, shoulders, or chest in case they should collide in midair and be forced to think fast."[1] The training to become a full-fledged action specialist is very similar.

In STREB's studio, there are no impossibilities. No mover utters the sentence, "That's not possible," or, "No, I can't do that." And you certainly can't say, "I don't want to." When I first asked one of STREB's major dancers, Hope Clark, who stayed with the company for close to ten years, to do something, after trying it she said, "Hmm, there are probably a couple of muscles that I might have to develop first to find my place in that particular space with those particular forces exploding around me." This was the perfect response. As Ivan and Noe Espana, our collaborators, often say to us, "Be afraid, be very afraid. That is what will keep you alive." The men and women I work with are true crusaders. They are modern-day gladiators. They seek what I call the holy grail of the real move. They know it exists, and every so often they experience it and the audience sees it. It's a sort of truth that doesn't occur in words or mathematical equations. It is undeniably a *Eureka!* moment.

POPACTION

This movement technique we work with and have developed over the past twenty years is called PopAction. That name comes from how we describe what it is that initiates a move. We say we pop our muscle groups, which then drag our skeletons around the stage. PopAction is not about transferring weight from one body part to another (this we see as a strictly predictable methodology called locomotion; it's what pedestrians do). We do not solely use the transfer method to produce any change of location. Our skeletons are a detail of our movement; ours is not a skeletal movement system. Our muscles drag our skeletons around. The first cause of human motion is a muscular explosion. PopAction is about exploding our bodies into the air all at once. If the execution of an action is predictive, we believe it will put the audience to sleep.

Unpredictable action is movement's equivalent to a page-turner in literature. On stage, we have certain options to make our moves appear surprising or even shocking. One choice is to remove transitions. We try to construct motion hunks, hunks of action that could be missed if an audience member blinks. A plié is a transition, a preparation, for a jump. Why bother jumping when the viewer knows in advance what the dancer is about to do? In STREB work, we don't plié—we fly, explode, gush into the air.

To be fair, some people create movement for aesthetic reasons. This sort of dancing seems more fun to do than to watch. But those are not the concerns of a real mover.

The body is the vessel for all human movement. Encoded in our brains from pre-birth are preconditions that surround the use of the body. These conditions or habits of use (or superstitions) are difficult even to notice, let alone change or eliminate. They are starkly different for each gender. I am writing on my experience of pushing the human body to the limits as a female, and what I have learned and suspected about the physical use of my body and the reactions to its use over the last twenty-five years and longer.

Many of my action heroes are willing to use their bodies in extreme ways. I have nothing but high regard for them. STREB shares this kind of action appetite. For me, two inspiring forces who transformed action are Merce Cunningham and Trisha Brown.

Merce was a spatial rhythmitician—he'd stab at the air unerringly, with the isolation of body parts that will not make a noise as the feet will when they stamp or land on the ground, guiding the body in its return from the air. By "air" I mean the area that lies invisibly above the ground. Most choreographers ignore or at the very least take for granted this vertical arena. His brilliance at commandeering space in an architectural manner demonstrated vividly that space is not as simple or benign as most dance-makers make it out to be. His ability to mechanize the function of the body was acutely compelling, merely by using the body against itself. The struggle, the intensity of this "againstness" made the drama and depth of his dances palpable. With no prejudice or sentimentality, Merce extracted the fundamentals of human motion. He took away all the unnecessary bits, all the flourishes, all the small lies we inadvertently tell with our supercilious gestures. These moves and gestures cloud the air and hamper our true stories from sounding through. Merce's movement, by contrast, told the truth.

No one in the dance world, in the new languages of the motion world, has been untouched by Trisha Brown's influence over the past forty years. Her brilliance is embedded in her relentless insistence that everything that came before is open to question, to reexamination. Trisha invented a new way to move on earth with the cliché-ridden human body—whether creating a performance spanning several Manhattan rooftops or employing computer technology to interact with the dancer's movements and the audience. She is the only choreographer who has redeployed the "where" of place and space, the "when" of time, and the "what" and "how" of the motion of the human form. Her formulas are still being deciphered by

us groundlings. Trisha took me, and all my cohorts, on a mystical journey through the tendrils of motion, necessity, and flight. Her work is the bedrock on which dance and movement of the twenty-first and twenty-second centuries will rest.

Other inspirations include Tehching Hsieh, the Espanas, Chris Burden, Gordon Matta-Clark, Evel Knievel, Muhammad Ali, The Flying Cranes, Harry Houdini, Annie Edson Taylor, Lynne Cox, Marina Abramovic, Zaha Hadid, Buster Keaton, Charlie Chaplin, The Three Stooges, Richard Serra, Nancy Grossman, Philippe Petit, Mikhail Baryshnikov, Craig Dykers, Snøhetta, Survival Research Laboratories, Mark Pauline, John Cage, and many unnamed circus performers. They were willing to go to great extremes to accomplish a real move. They saw the importance of their ambition and couldn't abandon it. They were willing to leave their mark on the earth, the sky, the water, and ultimately their own bodies, as a scarification of their flesh. Scarification occurs when we humans go a bit too close to the edge of our prescribed spaces, or arrive inaccurately temporally (at the wrong time), or in a way that doesn't fit the timing, place, and space required of a movement. It is like playing target practice with a whole body, and it's yours.

EXTREME ACTION SPECIALIST

I am more attracted to emergency actions than I am to volitional ones. I think it's critical to absorb and perfect a physical skill and become expert at it. I don't think this step can be skipped if you are to become a true action specialist. The task of choice comes when, after having been trained in a technique, you make a decision about whether to present those skills on stage (by exhibiting them), or alternatively, to use the skills within a constructed event designed to create turbulence and a certain amount of unpredictability due to the generation of particular forces. The goal for an extreme action specialist is to use your body as a vessel for the purpose of enduring these turbulent conditions, to exhibit determination, perseverance, and survival. An extreme action specialist designates her performance as an *event*, not a *presentation*. The distinction is that the former has a non-predictive outcome and the latter is meant to go perfectly as planned. A goal of *presenting* your acquired physical skill in this manner is a thinly veiled exposition of privilege. It would signify that you had the opportunity to train as a dancer for, say, twenty years. Someone paid for it, took you to and from classes all those years, believed in you, and participated in this social construct. I think that on a subconscious level, this is what gets noticed onstage by certain audience members, and it surreptitiously celebrates a class divide. It is partly responsible for the elite demographic that attends dance concerts, separate from how uninvited the general public feels vis-à-vis the act of entering a theater.

Action shows are events, not presentations. It is the difference between what you are actually *doing* or letting happen to your body, as opposed to what you are *showing* or *presenting*, which usually occurs in a more controlled or safe environment. The body is not engaged in showing the audience something, rather it is letting something extreme happen to it while an audience is present. One act exhibits courage and loss of self-interest, the other, solipsism.

Movement is an oral history, passed from one practitioner to another. What can that body do? And what marks are left behind on it after completion? What particular type of scarification? Is it merely a memory, or as a body moves with each move, does it create a more complete and physical marking of itself, internally if not externally? Is the history of moving embedded within each body? Does each body carry the content of its past actions? Is this, then, the true *meaning* of movement?

I can do what I do with my body because of its particular assets, shapes, muscles, proportions, and the other parts of my nature. The fact is, no one has the particular body I have. That is the premise of modern dance: the enormity of difference and the actions that different bodies invent. I do not just mean *invent*. Certain bodies and psyches are more willing than others to go to extreme places. Physicality is a conduit for the giving and receiving of harm, as well as pleasure.

I think the issue of class is deeply relevant in the practice of movement, yet very seldom does it get addressed. In everyday parlance, we see that ordinarily, the body as a human animal is protected by degrees of distance. The more privileged the person, the larger the yard, the higher the fence to protect them, and the more numerous the privacy laws which they deem necessary. The poorer a person is, the closer they come to physical harm, right up to the actual scarring of their skin, their faces, and their bodies.

Poor people have fewer means to keep harm at a distance, away from them; they have fewer means of protection. It's a crude valuation system.

The reason I choose to up the ante regarding extreme movement is that I believe that without danger and fear, movement is merely a decoration separate and apart from truth. STREB is all about the ugly, grubby, grunty aspects of movement. When my dancers walk into an action room, they agree to get hurt, to embrace danger. It is where the wild moments roam, but not without an inscriber—the body. Without the body, there is no actualization of real movement. I have always sought to measure just how much physicality the most exposed body could absorb: Is there a meter or scale to measure this type of intensity? Is there a method to ascertain the degree of magnitude? How much can the body take without dying? It could be similar to an IQ test. But it would measure a body's actual individual capacity, not only the body's potential average capacity.

We need a Richter scale for physical extremity. Is it of a greater intensity to have survived a plane crash, a bullet piercing you, or a building crashing down all around you? What can we use as our Richter scale for physical severity? Are the Niagara Falls heroes (such as Martha E. Wagenfuhrer), who got into a barrel and launched themselves over the Falls with very little planning or research, more extreme than Chuck Yeager, who flew the first plane to break the sound barrier? The Bell X-1 traveled at 761 mph! What was in his psyche as he climbed into the cockpit after being told by physicists that the plane would most likely disintegrate at those speeds? There is an act of will that allows

Martha E. Wagenfuhrer and her barrel, September 6, 1901.
Photo: Niagara Falls (Ontario) Public Library.

certain bodies to venture towards unknown outcomes. In my view, it is those particular humans who don't worry so much about themselves (or their well-being) who are truly brave. The unsentimental ones who design and perform moves that have such deep symbolism no one ever forgets them—those are my heroes, even if their actions only happen once. I am even willing to believe that conceptual extreme actions affect us psychically. For example, I am awed by what I believe Houdini did, and the courage his dares involved, whether or not he actually performed every act in the way he suggested he did.

I once saw a performer with the Moscow Circus drop 120 feet from a horizontal bar attached to the apex of the ceiling at Madison Square Garden. As he rose, attached by his wrist to a high-powered winch, four men stood beneath him, each holding an edge of a five-foot square mat that was about three feet thick, at about three or four feet from the ground. The four men and this pillow looked up as the performer rose, and they moved slightly, adjusting their position, trying to assess where exactly he would land once he returned to the ground, an almost impossible measuring problem. The performer's move was simply to let go, to perform a full-axial 360 degree swan dive and land on his feet, exactly in the middle of the mat. The second he landed, the four men released the catching-mat at *exactly the same instant,* a virtually impossible task. It dropped perfectly horizontally, and he landed vertically on the mat, with the mat and the man, at last, on the ground. Right after his touchdown, the performer rolled and ran. The audience was not prepared for this move. There was little fanfare, no advertisement (so unlike the circus, I thought). Even the memory of this move causes a rush of physical sensation throughout my body. I remember looking up, thinking no, don't, and then seeing him let go and fall. No act on earth is deeper than an act such as this, nothing short of death or murder.

STREB: Body

How do you practice such a move? Maybe ten feet at a time? No, it is a perfect example of a move for which you cannot rehearse. There is no practicing this move or marking out, a practice used in dance where dancers pretend to do the dance, walking through the space talking and pointing, mostly as a mental rehearsal. You just have to *do* it, or rather, *initiate* and then *let it happen.* Once you initiate it, you abandon all choice. Wait a moment too long, and you're history. Certainly this type of action constitutes a real move. And it also confirms another assessment quality of a real move: you'd get hurt trying to stop it.

People ask me how I feel about getting older as a dancer. Like most people, I think about mortality. I hope that reconciliation comes in the last half second of my life. When I'm taking my last breath, I want to look at how I used up the best of myself. How much did I sweat, push, pull, rip, fall, hit, crash, explode? My dream is to be so well used that in my last half second, I will burst into dust. This would signify that, in everything that had come before me in my life (all the seconds and all the acts), I had in fact completely and utterly used myself up, so that there would be nothing left to do but burst into dust with an enormous final force. To me, this would be physically responsible, and would reflect the perfecting of physical timing with matter, space, and body. It's a difficult thing to aspire to, and it can only be accomplished by a supreme action specialist.

SPACE

**It is possible to divide up the space inside
a sphere the size of a pea and rearrange it
so as to fill a sphere the size of the sun.**
—BANACH-TARSKI THEOREM

What constitutes being in space? How do bodies absorb movement? How can a gravity-bound body accomplish the act of actually, authentically occupying space?

I've never jumped out of an airplane. I didn't think this act would give me a good idea of what the nature of space might be. I have jumped off a ladder and crashed onto a hardwood floor. I felt the terrible, horrible effect of gravity as I hit the ground. But for a second right after jumping, I was flying, truly midair. Then *whammo!* Meet the monster, the ugly part of our world—gravity—and all its other force-field friends: inertia, rebound, impact, adhesion, centripetal force, momentum, velocity, acceleration, and dead stops. This thing called gravity is what all motion genres avoid even acknowledging; certainly dance, ballet, and the circus spend a lot of time camouflaging its effect. Only football, rodeo, boxing, and World Wrestling Entertainment are unafraid of this force, the weakest one we have on earth.

In my introduction I mention my bike trip across America, during which I passed through the most enormous hunk of space in one time period that I could ever have conceived of. I was utterly unprotected. My body was whizzing at seventy mph across and through six thousand contiguous miles of the good ol' US of A. There was absolutely nothing abstract or postmodern about that ride. My father, Leonard, wanted me to take mace and a gun for protection. It was cheaper than getting me health insurance. He claimed that you couldn't use a weapon on another person unless you fully understand the effect you/it will cause. He said you have to shoot yourself and mace yourself first. I left the gun at home, with him.

I bought this particular motorcycle while in college in 1970, the year my mother tragically died. This sudden loss blasted out my heart. I took some drugs and drove my bike recklessly. This was my third motorcycle, and my last. For nine years, from age fifteen to twenty-four, the bike defined me. I felt I was a beatnik, a bohemian; a hood, not a hippie, not even a little.

I would upset my college roommates by riding my motorcycle up the stairs into my small bedroom, to keep it safe and dry for the winter months. I can't remember how I got the bike downstairs when the spring came. But the ride up felt transgressive, clearly very disturbing to everyone, and this feeling, this awareness, was interesting to me. I was unconsciously gathering critical physical information about it. Curious, I thought, why certain behavior, certain actions are upsetting.

In 1972 there were floods up and down the East Coast, and all phone service was out. I had planned to ride across country with Cathy Sample, a friend from college who lived in Corning, New York, who also had a 350 Honda. There was no way to contact her about our departure. I was ready to go, so one morning I rode out of Rochester, New York, never to return, and a few hours later I found her at home. She was not surprised to see me. I said, "Let's go." She got all her stuff sorted out, said goodbye to her family, and we left, heading to New Orleans. I think this decision was based on having just seen the film *Easy Rider*. It was severely illogical, since I was going to San Francisco. Cathy was going no place in particular. We started squabbling early on. She wouldn't ride in the rain; I would. She wasn't in a hurry; I was. By the time we passed through Houston, we split up. So there I was, twenty-two years old, riding alone across the longest set of roads I had ever seen. They get a lot longer when there is not much to separate you and the road. I don't remember much. I didn't stay in hotels, I'd wait for the sun to almost set, and for there to be no cars in either direction. Then I would pull off the road and ride up into some bushes or rock formations, trying not to make a dust trail, lay my bike down, get out my sleeping bag, and go to sleep. I had given Cathy the tent.

Now I look at the seats of motorcycles and cannot believe I took off the way I did. I had about two hundred dollars with me that I earned in Rochester and about seventy dollars left by the time I arrived in San Francisco. It was 10 a.m. on a Tuesday morning, 1972. I had brought with me the address of a health food store; someone said it had a corkboard with room listings. A guy named Ira Bruckner was there looking at the same board. I had my helmet with me and my bike parked outside with all my stuff— paintings and dance clothes. On the way across country,

I told anyone who would listen that I was a dancer and an artist, and was headed to California to begin my professional journey. Ira said he had a room with two beds in it for thirty-five dollars a month; he would split it with me. Cool. Day one solved.

My father was supposed to send me my last check from my mother's social security reimbursement (each kid got seventy-four dollars a month until they left school). My sister Lori never went to school, so only I got the money. He said he couldn't front it to me and that he'd send it general delivery to the San Francisco Post Office. Every day I went to the post office to see if it came. With the rest of my money I bought a month's worth of classes at the Margaret Jenkins Studio and at the San Francisco Ballet School. I would take two classes every day for the remainder of my dance training, which ended in 1995 when I was forty-five.

These stark beginnings taught me many things. One of the conditions of personhood, especially critical for young women, is to not worry about the future, and certainly to not worry about yourself. You have to risk everything at least once, dive into a city with some but not a lot of money, and, knowing no one, begin your life anew. In a fundamental way, it's about learning to take up space.

In past eras, movement held a different status. Movement simply allowed you to stay alive. Fundamentally, life and death hinged on noticing physical activities that were the harbingers of disaster. For instance, the erratic way small animals move is often dangerous: think of a rattlesnake, or the brown recluse spider, whose sudden attack can be fatal.

Skills of paying attention to physical phenomena proved to be a Darwinian advantage. Once upon a time, humans had a more conscious relationship to the senses and to our bodies vis-à-vis the physical world and its shiftings. The ability of the eye and the mind to take in the physical world was paramount.

In my practice, I'm trying to return to a time before text, to when movement meant all there was to mean. When the concern for establishing content in movement was relegated to simply staying alive. Now, content in movement is often referential or descriptive or emotional: how artificial, how unnecessary.

As a choreographer, I want to affect space through action—extreme action—in such a way that the audience notices the subject of what I am doing, which is to say, the subject of action. Usually what people notice is its implementer, the body. My stock and trade is to present action as subject, not body as object. But it is very difficult to get a human being's attention away from the human form. I want the audience to notice where the body is going, or has been, and perhaps wonder where it will go next. But certainly not merely what it is doing. It's not what you do, it's where you go. I want them to notice what happens *because* of the doing and *not* the doing itself. Watching *what* the body is doing will never allow us to remove our attention from the body. Therefore, we will not notice its effect on space and we won't experience movement. This is a subtle distinction. It's hard not to care what the body looks like; it is a human habit to care about our bodies. That is why the movement must be extreme, very extreme.

"Drop," a bungee cord dance from "Action Heroes," 2000. Photo: Tom Caravaglia.

ARENA

This idea of shifting the focus is most clearly understood in a very short physical event, like falling from a quite high place. In this situation, if your attention is on the body, you as a viewer won't experience the fall. My goal, then, is to affect a paradigm shift in the audience's attention. One of my primary challenges is to consider space. I am referring here to the artificial space of the theater, not outside space, although I think that we humans tend to reference space in an assortment of inaccurate ways. When a movement artist enters this artificial space (the space of the theater), an examination needs to occur. How does the choreographer format this arena within its obvious limitations? First, one can't ignore outside space: the sky, the oceans, the land, outer space, and moon-like space—the places that typically demarcate human location. Those are the non-trivial, irreducible arenas to which we have access and which constitute and control all of our perceptions of place in this world. I once heard astronaut Story Musgrave speak at a NASA convention in Washington DC, and he explained that in space, up and down immediately disappear as concepts, and this confounds every thought you have for quite a while because "where we are" is a knowledge necessary to "what we think."

Even if they exist only in our mind's eye, every place we inhabit (including the stage) will be compared to outside space. What is the format, proportion, scale, design, or frame of reference of action's container?

Other live-time arts have attended to the problem, or question, of space by tailoring their use of theatrical space in a diligent and formal way. I don't believe dance has done that. What ought to be the design of action's presentational place? We have to ask (and answer) the question before we decide on our first move. Where is the mover? What is the nature of the particular place in space I have chosen to occupy? How do I define and tailor space to increase the chance that what I am doing will be noticed?

The design of the proscenium that typically frames an opera stage isn't random, it has a very specific aspect ratio. The design and proportion of what we know as the proscenium have everything to do with the grandiose sets and painted drops employed to add spectacle to the operatic event. To accommodate those sets and drops, the opera stage is by necessity huge in terms of cubic dimension. To balance the relatively tiny size of a human in the vastness of such a stage, opera directors put masses of people on stage. Designers of symphony stages employ sound scientists to attend to the acoustics so that every string plucked or note blown is audible to the audience member in the last row of the highest balcony of the concert hall.

How should the dance world design the presenting arena that might most fundamentally and critically fulfill its needs for movement? What is our version of absolute silence, and how can our space accommodate it? What would be its height or shape or footprint? Would dance's platform of presentation be a turning surface, so that at each moment the audience would be experiencing a different angle of viewing, creating more dimensions to the viewers' experience? Dance needs to not merely fit itself into whatever space happens to be available.

STREB: Space

Think about it. Pioneer filmmakers selected a particular aspect ratio for their screen. The inventors of television chose a different screen shape (which is why many films have to be reformatted for television broadcast). Actually, I have always wondered why every presentation space—technological or live-time—selects a particular aspect ratio, and why it is always either rectangular or square. Even in the circus there are functional reasons behind the choices made for the circus tent and its shape. They decided that their arena needed to be a circle. It is economically smart. You can have more higher-priced seats if you can fit more people closer to the action. And it is more equitable than a rectangular seating area because there are more front seats relative to the so-called peanut gallery.

What defined the diameter of the circus ring? The traditional ring is twenty-two feet in diameter for a reason. Twenty-two feet is the turning ratio required for horses to run fast enough for riders to stand up on them (which is to say, at a smooth canter rather than a rocky trot). There is nothing arbitrary about this decision. What is dance's version of this deep functionality?

Movement artists (dancers and choreographers) have always settled for already existing places: opera houses, theater stages, or music halls. Movement artists have used presentation spaces designed by others, for other disciplines. As a result, when dancers work on stage, the majority of the available visual space, the vacant twenty feet above performers' heads, is empty, not used, and mostly ignored. As Le Corbusier said, "The size and relative proportionality of the human has to be quantified."[1] But it's as

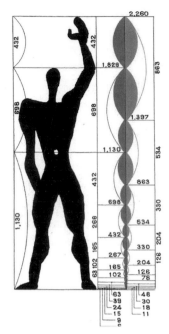

A scale for the harmonic measurement of space from Le Corbusier's *Modular 2*.

if choreographers conceded immediately to the structures of other forms, and said, perhaps subconsciously, "I can't change the action space, so I'll just throw some lights on the cyclorama and get on with what I am doing on the ground."

I want to be more specific and accurate about movement stages. I am inclined to believe that, as in the circus, the presentation of movement needs to take place in a circle, and that the ideal circular platform would continuously turn at a slow, almost undecipherable rate.

I have designed the STREB stage to be twenty feet across and to contain eight dancers. A twenty-foot square is just enough, and more importantly, not too much space, for eight humans to affect an audience with action, given the current size of the human form. I came to this conclusion taking clues and information from other fields. I thought about certain mathematical equations and considered the principles of movement in visual arts. In thinking about minimalism, I wondered what new, simple, and essential idea I could perform that would say it all about space. Could I perform the idea of a line? I recognized impressionism in my work in the fuzzy borders, or blur, created in a real move. The need for a hard edge or exposing the idea of position was not of interest to me. In terms of appropriation, I collected motions from other sources that were not strictly "dance" sources, such as slapstick, accidents, and labor. I borrowed methods and styles applied to architecture, such as Le Corbusier's idea of coding spatial harmonics from nature, using the golden ratio or the golden mean, and coefficients of restitution when contending with impact. I utilized certain physics formulas that told the truth about causality and natural objects. Nature has a phenomenal array of secrets to share that we need to borrow and employ choreographically.

UN-HABITUAL SPACE

When one walks into a room or ventures outside, the relative vastness of all the spatial terrain one does *not* occupy can be overwhelming. Given all *other* space (where we are not), there are choices to be made. One option is to ignore the true nature of space and pretend that you are responsible only for the area that is already easily accessible to you. The other is to explore un-habitual space by getting off the ground. Typically, our bodies occupy space vertically, i.e., right side up with the weight on the bottom of one's feet. By un-habitual space I'm referring to the space occupied when the body is not vertical. In un-habitual space, the body experiences discomfort and often confusion, mostly due to the lack of particular sensations that gravity and motion provoke. Choosing the latter involves other necessary

"Fly," Coney Island, NY, 1998.

questions: where, in un-habitual space, do you want to go? Directions and choices increase and become bewildering when the space one chooses to occupy ceases to be two-dimensional, and one abandons the hegemony of the ground and standing upright.

Is it possible to choose a place in space that no one has *ever* occupied in exactly that particular way before? Such a decision—to design and locate an *un-habitual place in space*—makes it possible not only to change our own actual place in space, it also opens up the possibility of tilting, twisting, and turning space to reorient the audience's sense of where they are. Then the audience's physical perceptions corrupt their ordinary view. The act of changing where we are as dancers can provide audiences, for example, with a bird's-eye view or an eagle's-eye view (a high-up or even higher-up perspective) or a worm's-eye view (seeing everything from below). We can even create a possum's-eye view, (everything is, or appears to be, upside down) or a fly's-eye view (where everything becomes jittery).

PERSPECTIVE

The idea of designing differing eye view perspectives is an important device choreographically in regards to the formal use of space. I want to make the audience feel located in different places at varying times throughout the extreme action show; my goal is to make them feel as if they have had an extreme physical experience. To accomplish this goal, I must create a change in the audience's orientation because of the change in the performers'. It's odd how this happens. For instance, in the STREB performance "LookUp," the dancers have switched their ground to a large, thirty by thirty-feet perpendicular wall. They don gyroscopic harnesses and attach these harnesses to a cable system coming out from the top of the wall, and then plant their feet on this wall at a ninety degree angle. The audience begins to feel as if they are looking down onto the heads of the dancers. Clearly the audience has not moved, yet they feel lifted above the dancers, who were the ones who actually changed their places in space, not the audience. The dominion of space demands that the perspective of the viewer rights itself and somehow makes sense of what cannot be: people can't walk on walls. So even the dancers actually walking on walls is not convincing; we are not able to be that spatially flexible. The audience will pretend that

"LookUp" at the Museum of Contemporary Art, Los Angeles, CA, 1995. Photos: Kevin Adams.

STREB: Space

the dancers are still on the ground, even if the performance shifts them mysteriously above or below them depending on how close the audience is to the performers. This seems a more reasonable approach in the effort to make sense out of what they are perceiving. The photos of "LookUp" clarify this phenomenon.

The use of space is not casual; it is critical. As problematic as the theatrical stage is for action, theatrical stages at least frame human movement in a less competitive way than outside or outdoor space does. Outside, movers must contend with an unmanageable scale problem: the human-sized person against a backdrop of clouds. As noted in *The Deleuze Dictionary*, "Space is rich in potentiality because it makes possible the realization of events. A given image or concept, when it is seen or engaged, creates and dissipates space in the time of its perception. Space is something that is at the edges of language. Deleuze calls the apprehension of space an 'exhaustion' of meaning."[2] Once space is used as a crossing zone for movement, it loses its criticality, it returns to invisibility, a useless vessel. Space gets noticed when it actually becomes occupied by an extreme move within it, not moving through it. A perfect example of what I see as a waste of space is the ubiquitous step-step-leap which is used liberally when a choreographer wants to get a dancer off the stage. A more interesting venture, in my opinion, would be to ask, what do I really want to happen physically right *now*? The answer might be, I want the dancer to disappear. Then I suggest trying to figure out how to make that happen physically, rather than saying first off, oh, that's impossible.

"Lake Sunapee Dive, New Hampshire," 1972. Photo: Terry Wild.

PERCEPTION OF MOVEMENT

In this regard, I think of Kant's argument for the non-trivial and a priori existence of space. I see this as a great exercise, at the very least to encourage choreographers (in this case, me) to contend seriously with space when constructing movement events. Kant begins his argument with the assertion that "space is not an empirical concept that has been drawn from outer experiences." He continues:

> In order for certain sensations to be related to something outside me (i.e., to something in another place in space from that in which I find myself), thus in order for me to represent them as outside and next to one another, thus not merely as different but as in different places, the representation of space must already be their ground. Thus the representation of space cannot be obtained from the relations of outer appearance through experience, but this outer experience is itself first possible only through this representation.[3]

Kant states that it is not the relation of objects to one another that establishes them as being in space, but rather the context of space that we bring to every experience. This cannot be an act of our will.

In part, this idea regarding space seems intuitively right, but the explanation seems contingent on our experience of space being purely visual, or two-dimensional. The true nature of space and how and when it operates is a slippery subject. I cannot separate it from the things that happen within it. I contend that the visual experience and the aural experience are the predominant ones operating in the current proscenium presentation. And I want movement, a physical form, to be experienced as physical first, which requires the recognition of more than two dimensions. Jonathan Bennett explains:

> If we had to choose between a visual and a tactual-kinaesthetic basis for spatial concepts, we should choose the latter. The reason for this is also the reason why tactual-kinaesthetic considerations *are now* more central to our spatial concepts than are visual considerations, even though the two roughly coincide: since physical contact is involved in all the main ways in which things can hurt, soothe, nourish or protect us, the "Where?" which matters most is the tactual-kinaesthetic "Where?" which asks how to achieve or avoid physical contact. Visual fields are quick, reliable and fairly comprehensive guides to the spatial relations amongst physical things; but they have this virtue only because they correlate with those tactual and kinaesthetic facts which lie at the heart of our concept of physical space.[4]

In fact, visual cues allow us to grasp and make sense of a picture intellectually; they give us a fully reliable sense of what is where in space. But is the tactual-kinaesthetic "Where?" what tips us off best? As my partner says, "The stop sign is less effective than a hole in the road." This is what we obsess over when it comes to constructing a physical movement: How can we control how the audience perceives the action event, to feel the experience first, before seeing it?

While observing the photograph on the next page, for instance, something helps me to know that what appears

"Casino Pool, Lake Worth, FL," 1978. Photo: Jerry Gordon.

to be a very small body growing out of one person's head is, in fact, a diver jumping into a swimming pool far in the distance. Something helps me, the observer, to understand that distance between two objects separates them spatially. I am able to understand that they are not the same object, nor are they in the same space, and I can confirm that if I am actually there, not just observing a photograph, by doing a physical and tactile test, in other words, by walking up to things and touching them.

Perhaps "separating spaces" need to be treated differently from the space an object occupies. An audience member cannot get up and double check to see if their eyes are deceiving them by walking on stage and investigating the distances. As the choreographer who has (perhaps inadvertently) constructed this stage picture, I take seriously that the audience may very well perceive the equivalent of the (far-off) small diver and the (close-up) big head as existing in the same space. It is the audience's job to deconstruct this nonsensical image in a meaningful way.

Framing action consciously (rather than making unexamined assumptions about the where, how, what, and when of stage-space) demands a certain methodology. In my practice, it requires a particular set of techniques to deliver the experience of a real move to an audience. These devices, techniques, or tools are necessary to arrive at the possibility of a real move, a move that the audience will experience without any doubt about what the move is, or how the movement affects them (even if they have no name for it).

The devices I include here constitute the various frames of reference that must be mapped out in order to look at or experience action more effectively. For one thing, we need to choose and define action's vanishing point. The vanishing point was discovered long ago for the visual arts (specifically, for painting, by Filippo Brunelleschi, in the fifteenth century). No such agreement has been reached on action's vanishing point. Could the vanishing point for action be where the horizontal crashes into the vertical (otherwise known as the horizon line)? After all, the horizon line is the great space separator: it conjoins the horizontal spaces we know so well to the vertical, the ground and the sky. It is how we humans typically get our bearings; this is the place where the land hits the sky. The sculptor Richard Serra said, reflecting on a Barnett Newman painting, "It could be that the vertical in relation to the horizontal field is fundamental to how we perceive and understand time, place, and space;

that he touched upon something that has to do with how we move and how we think when we move . . ."[5] This is how we humans understand spatially what we are actually *perceiving*, and more critically, where we *are* at any particular moment in time and where the rest of the world is. It is necessary to understand how our eyes and brains make automatic separations in the space we gaze out into.

There are other tools, along with the horizon line, that if noticed and employed, we can use to create more articulate staged action events. Parallax view is the phenomenon that causes objects to appear to change when viewed from different locations. For example, objects closer to the viewer seem to move more rapidly than objects further away. As viewers change their angle of viewing, the backgrounds of the objects also appear to change almost as if they, the objects, have either moved or somehow have been transported magically to a different place in space. These occurrences result in what we see and perceive. They happen so rapidly, and we are so used to them, that they require deconstruction in order for us to name them and understand their usefulness.

At the moment we plant our gaze, parallax view helps us separate our right and left vision frames just as the horizon line separates top from bottom or vertical from horizontal. If you think your left eye sees exactly what your right eye sees, then cover one eye, then the other, and notice your error. In a similar way, when it comes to seeing action, the horizon line might also be considered to divide our field of vision, but in the other direction. This sort of information is useful to consider before we are able to

"Airlines," 1987, 2009. "Airlines" is a Mondrian-like manifestation of a series of cubicles that designate the various areas in which the average human body can reside. There are a total of eighteen areas depicted by this grid. The performance of

"Airlines" constitutes various entrances and exits from a variety of occupations by different numbers of dancers at any one time. This grid is attached to a floor which slowly turns as the dancers perform.

"PolarWander," 2009. This is a dance featuring a heavy, sharp, eight-foot-long steel I-beam. It is connected to a cable that rises and lowers as the I-beam spins. It's an escape game that demonstrates the pure, perfect, and authentic timing of circular motion.

"Artificial Gravity," 2009. This floor was designed with two separate turning surfaces, each powered by a different motor. It creates a sideways turbulence and forces not possible to access with the mechanics of the human body. ES choreographs certain maneuvers attempting to demonstrate the beauty of the circle as it forces an object to return to its origin by merely staying where it already is as well as attempting to create the illusion of bodies occupying the same place at the same time.

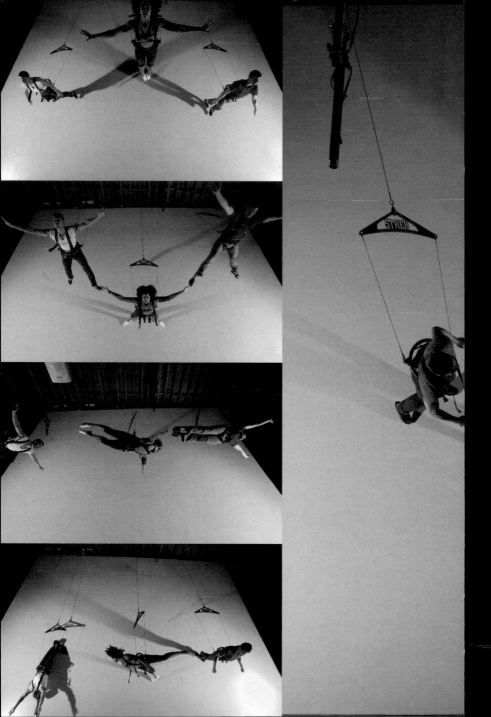

"RunUpWalls," 2010. This dance occurs on a twenty-five-by-twenty-five-foot vertical wall. The dancers are counterweighted by one another: when one rushes up, the other hurls down. The distance of the drop or the rise can be covered in an instant. The rising body defies gravity and the falling body is subject to its speed and force, thirty-two-foot-per-second squared.

"Wild Blue Yonder," 2003–04.
STREB was commissioned by Wolf Trap to perform at the celebration commemorating the one hundredth anniversary of the Wright Brothers flight in Kitty Hawk, North Carolina. These photos are taken during the making of this show, when STREB was "in residence" on the actual sands of Kitty Hawk attempting to demonstrate a twelve-second version of their continuous flight. They flew and fell on these hallowed grounds.

"SuperPosition," 2009. This device was designed and built by Noe and Ivan Espana. The circle rotates with a counterweight at the other end, and at a particular moment in its revolution achieves an antigravity space-time moment. It passes as a large wave in the ocean does, in a nanosecond. The body has to be ready to ride it out.

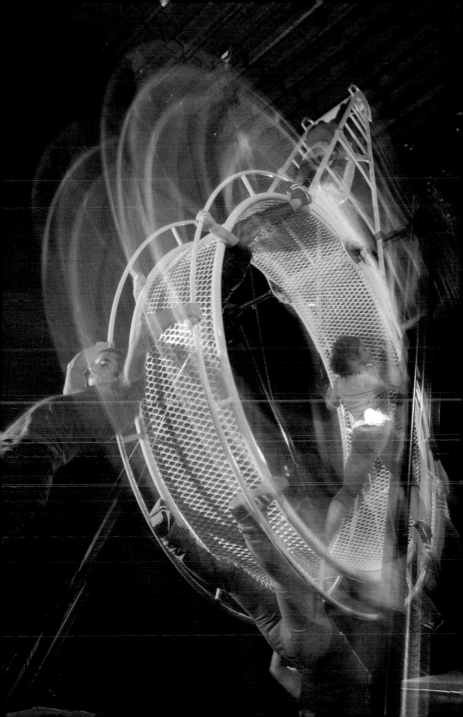

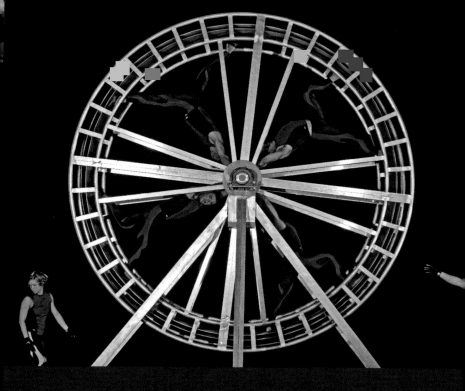

ABOVE: "Revolution," 2006. This equipment was conceived by ES and designed by Michael Casselli. It is essentially a human-sized hamster wheel. It weighs two tons and is accelerated by the running, moving, or flying bodies that mount it, get in, and fly off through a very small triangle. These entrances and exits occur as the giant wheel mercilessly whizzes by.

OPPOSITE TOP: "Ricochet," 2006. A vertical, nine-by-nine-foot Plexiglas surface structurally attached to the building it is performed in. Eight bodies hurl themselves with full human force at both sides of the Plexiglas wall. For a few precious seconds—caused by adhesion, cohesion, and momentum—these bodies are allowed to achieve unbelievable positions in space and time. The predominant subject is impact and the intensity of the hit.

OPPOSITE BOTTOM: "Orbit," 2006. Two dancers attached to rope tethered to the top of a circus pole, wind and unwind around it. The forces generated by these simple, childlike actions are substantive enough to affect a thick space-time orbital motion, within which the dancers flip, spin, and ride one another until the forces of the spin erode. This erosion releases them either onto the circular ground of the pole or back down to earth.

"Gauntlet," 2004. This dance was commissioned by Jazz at Lincoln Center for their opening celebration. ES hung two ninety-pound cement blocks on two different length cables attached high above the ground. Due to their different lengths, two distinct swing durations cause eccentric temporal intersections. As they were swung throughout the seven-minute dance, the eight dancers ran, dove, ducked and maneuvered themselves ever away from the insistent pathways of these small, yet crushing devices.

COLOR PHOTOS BY TOM CARAVAGLIA

truly comprehend physical experience. The organization of human action events is riddled with many formal conditions. We are responsible for understanding perception, and are forced to make decisions that can adjust the viewers' experiences of what we are doing and what happens to the viewers when our extreme actions are performed.

To recap, real moves happen in un-habitual places in space and demand special means (new hardware devices, perhaps) to get into those places. In order to be effectively perceived, notion in space requires a clear, consciously designed frame, a frame that surrounds it and serves to formalize the activity of the dancers, attending to relative size and proportion. Other critical factors include careful use of angles of view and action's vanishing point (the horizon line), and its left to right space separator contained in the phenomena of parallax view. Now the body must get off the ground and learn to fly!

A bit of crazy magic has to occur. We at STREB are not pretending that the forces that hold us down are not real and powerful. We are taking that fact into account and still attempting to launch our bodies up. This invective holds within it the understanding that there are many and varied ways to fly. Bodies that agree to fly also must agree not only to get off the ground, but also to return to it eventually. They have to be willing to be victims of the forces that govern heavy objects on and off the earth. If the first prerogative is to wrest ourselves from the hegemony of the ground then you have to get up into the air somehow. This will entail embracing fear and the conditions of danger.

Getting away from the earth (or off the ground) forces a body to be in an un-habitual place in space, as mentioned earlier. This describes body orientation, base of support, and spatial location. Once the body is off the ground, it does not encounter stasis or stillness. (But clearly the act of standing still requires the function of thousands of constant propriocentric adjustments!) The body can't stand still, or be still, off the ground. A person off the ground cannot initiate movement. Even if, in reference to one's own body, one seems not to be moving, the physical reality is that one *is* moving, back down to the earth, at thirty-two feet per second squared, otherwise known as falling. In addition, we know that planet Earth, depending on the latitude you measure from, is hurtling through space at sixty thousand miles per hour.

In making this point, I am massively simplifying all conditions of relative motion. (The fact is, there is no absolute stillness; everything is always turning and hurtling through space, but on earth, we experience stillness nonetheless because the distances moved are so great and the movement so imperceptible to our sensors and our gaze.) If you accept the premise that in order to truly, *really*, move you cannot be on the ground or in a known or comfort-based position, then the imagining begins. The goal is to not just perform meta-movements such as ballet's port de bras or développés or even step-step-leap, but a real move at last. You can't *do* real movement; it has to happen to you. Normative movements of ballet require an extraordinary degree of physical skill, and performing them seems like the exhibition of that skill, not of ripping through space and tak-

A "heel drive," Coney Island, NY, 1999.

ing on what it means to truly move through time with the body as implementer dealing with the forces that propel it.

How do we humans leave the ground? How do we get up into the air? A person could choose to jump up. In *The Universe in a Teacup*, K.C. Cole mentions cryptically that "all animals jump to about the same height off the ground—about 3 feet (one meter)—whether a human, a flea, or a cat."[6] In my view, jumping three feet is not high enough or does not last long enough to be able to *do* anything that a person watching might notice, especially if the jumper remains in a vertical position, with feet underneath the body, perpendicular to the earth (remember, I am always referring to constructing an effective yet artificial theatrical action event). If, on the other hand, you did what STREB calls a "heel drive" at the initiation of the jump—forcing your legs behind you, utilizing a rabidly fast and accurate explosion backward with the heels of both feet, which are mostly stuck together, and at the very same instant taking the torso (top half) forward; positioning yourself now horizontally to the ground, facing down, stomach parallel to the earth, causing a horizontal line in your entire body, using the same balletic alignment as when vertical—feet, knees, stomach, shoulders, ears—then you will have a bit longer to fall back to earth. Maybe it's true that you have traveled no higher, but at least you made your entire self travel further from the ground, in that you've taken your whole body to the height that your hips once were (and essentially still are). In this case, now you might squeeze in a couple more moves, in addition to the one you performed to get your body into the horizontal plane in the first place. For instance, you could perform a horizontal 360 degree or even a 540 degree and land on your back! This event may last only a fraction of a second, but it is a very short experience of true flight.

When a body walks into a room, or finds itself standing on the earth in a traditional way, no real moves can occur. No curiosities or serious queries about the nature of space, or the body's place in space, or what position it takes within that space, will ever be encountered. You are feeling the same physical feeling you always do, so much so that long ago you stopped feeling it at all. This is the effect of a physical cliché. Your very being in space, in the vertical way you exist, has become a habit. The problem with a physical cliché, with all clichés, is that we, you, do not notice them. All feeling, as well as comprehension, has abandoned the body. For instance, if you lay down horizontally for ten years and then went to stand up, you'd surely recognize

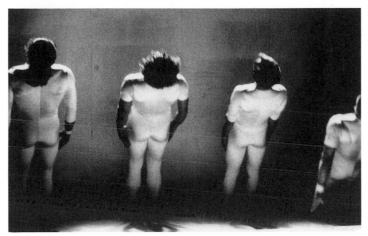

A "back fall" during the Bessie Awards ceremony, Brooklyn Academy of Music, NY, 1990–91. Photo: Scott Heiser

how radical standing up and balancing on the relatively minute surface area found on the bottoms of your feet is. So at STREB, where we want to recognize the idea and experience of space, an investigative process about space has to be the first order of business.

Some radical movements can occur close to the ground and be fairly simple, such as the "back fall." In early 1989 I tried this after watching a piece of plywood fall to the floor. I wondered if I could make myself be perfectly straight and *stay* aligned as I went off my right-angle orientation toward the ground and the forces started to assail my body and mind. It was very difficult physically, emotionally, and psychologically. I buckled and panicked, trying to save myself because of my ingrained reactions to how wrong falling backward feels. I was whiplashed many times but finally, I got it right! This is a perfect example of an anti-intuitive move. I did this before we used mats. The mats were introduced in 1990 with a piece called "Spacehold."

The first step I take is to figure out how to get into and be in that space we have designed and structured in a real way. The next step, once we are there in the designated space that we have clearly designed, entered, and occupied, is to develop the physical vocabulary particular to that space. One of the methods used to align with this investigation is to create hundreds of drawings, which help me imagine what might be possible there. We begin to invent, heuristically, the infinite number of moves that can be accommodated by that very specific place in space (and none other). When you change your place in space, new moves become more possible than before, and even look and feel different to the practitioner and also to the observer. It is here, after all the spatial occupational decisions have occurred, that the action vocabulary is discovered. If you think of the standard dance studio as a place for a dance to be invented, then we at STREB think of every one of our physical contraptions as a new design for a new kind of dance studio, but with a completely different set of conditions. A dance studio contains the same amount of space, time, and forces no matter when you walk into it. It has a perfectly horizontal hardwood floor, usually with mirrors in which dancers check out their positions, and it has a ballet barre. Often, no food, drinks, or shoes are allowed into the studio. At the time in my life when I thought that this was the only space to invent action in, I was very forlorn. What could a body do in such a sterile environment? How could you fly here?

ACTION MACHINES

Space appears empty, but it is not. It contains forces, which are also invisible, and these forces operate on the hard objects that encounter them. Of these forces, gravity is the most noticeable. It is quite easy to stay on the ground, rabidly difficult to leave it.

Gilles Deleuze states:

> If things endure, or if there is duration in things, the question of space will need to be reassessed on new foundations. For space will no longer simply be a form of exteriority, a sort of screen that denatures duration, an impurity that comes to disturb the pure, a relative that is opposed to the absolute: space itself will need to be based in things, in relations between things and between durations, to belong itself to the absolute, to have its own "purity."[7]

Is the addition of relations between things and durations equal to movement? Or would it be the intersection of these two aspects of reality and phenomena? Is this where we find the ineffable idea called time?

One method to try to define more articulately the contours of space (the shape of space) is to shift the surface of one's ground away from the way it is naturally experienced by using a machine. The Wright Brothers exclaimed during their experiments with manned flight machines: "If you are looking for perfect safety you will do well to sit on a fence and watch the birds, but if you wish to learn, you must mount a machine and become acquainted with its tricks."[8]

"Revolution," 2006.
Photo: Tom Caravaglia.

Access to a new place or situation in space usually requires a new piece of specially designed action equipment or Action Machines. The Action Machines at STREB—the wall, fly machine, bungees, wheels, boxer harnesses, plywood, pipe-grids, walls, and trampolines—are our spaceships. They enable us to travel to unknown, un-traversed topographies. These beautiful action contraptions are our ground-shifters and force-implementers. In order to change our place in space, I borrow a methodology from scientists, most notably a process akin to what Einstein called "thought exercises" (for me they are often drawing exercises). I work on the problem of what the next action contraption might be, often for a couple of years before I build anything. I work with technical directors to think through and design the details of what the hardware contraptions might function as and look like, design-wise. Through the years, I have worked with Bill Ballou, Michael Casselli, Phil Crowder, Justin D'Apalito, my longtime collaborators Noe and Ivan Espana, and STREB's current technical designer, Aaron Verdery. I call these guys (so far, all guys!) Hardware Junkies.

Once a design is set, I then go into rehearsal to create the new vocabulary that emerges from traveling to these new territories, aided by our new machines. STREB Action Machines are akin to musical instruments. I imagine that long ago, someone must have suspected and believed that the human voice alone was not sufficient to express all that sound seems capable of. And so the harpsichord, the flute, and the horn were invented. What would be the equivalent idea to tone, pitch, harmony, and melody in movement?

I develop the ideas for machines to help me address my first question about space: Where have I not yet been? Of course, there is irony in posing this question. Clearly you can't know where you have not been if these places have no name. When I asked Lisa Randall, a leading theoretical physicist, what the six extra dimensions posited in superstring theory would do to a body if they were scaled up and not hidden, she said "If they existed, these dimensions would already be all over us right now; we wouldn't be able to see them because they *are* hidden—either infinitesimally small or ever large—but warped." This helps me to understand that there is so much to the physical world—and certainly to motion and space and time—that is all around us, but we simply are not equipped to notice. We have to create the conditions to notice new aspects of our physical world. One of the ways STREB attempts to accomplish this is by the invention of Action Machines.

The machines we invent do not just serve to get us into certain places. The new "spots" in space that we explore are also laden with forces (and place us in conditions which produce forces) that we can harness. In a human-size hamster wheel, for example, movers find themselves not only in an un-habitual space, but also subject to particular forces (centripetal, torque, impact, rebound) enabling them to invent certain moves. For example, some of these forces allow break-dancers to switch their base of support from their hands to their heads and then back to their feet again. By always turning, break-dancers are able to go faster and faster, and it's in this faster "circling zone" that the magic of action, and its compressed space-time, transpires.

STREB: Space

"Revolution," 2006. Photo: Tom Caravaglia.

I want our performances to be events of desire and purpose, not presentations of skill that could easily read as privilege. I want the STREB Extreme Action performances to do something to the audience, to cause a physical reaction so strong that they feel that some of the moves have literally happened to them. So the situation manufactured by these mechanical and functional (not theatrical) sets produces a turbulent condition that the dancers have to figure out how to navigate. Anyone who has ever tried to travel faster than the speed of sound, like Chuck Yeager, knows that it's not just about where you are, but what's happening to you as you arrive there and exactly what conditions exist there.

"Artificial Gravity," 2009. Photo: Tom Caravaglia.

Consider a prototype used in a STREB piece titled "Artificial Gravity." The machine features a twenty-foot circular floor with an eight-foot-wide circle in its center, surrounded by a six-foot donut. Each section of the floor is attached to a beefy motor. One motor allows the eight-foot disc to rotate clockwise or counterclockwise at varying speeds, and the other allows the donut that surrounds it to do the same. Rounding down the π ratio to 3 (not 3.14) and calculating the circumference (or distance) represented by this circle, the disc has a radius of approximately four feet. Its circumference, then, is $2\pi \times r$, which equals about twenty-five feet. That's a long distance, especially since the circle is actually only eight feet across! By the same token, the circumference of the donut would be about sixty feet. The entire stage of STREB is only twenty square feet. So just by making this same distance curve, I gain a lot of space.

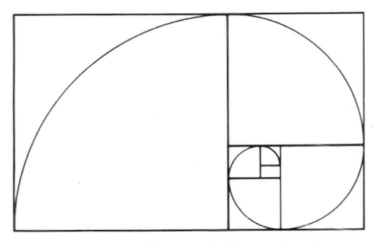

A Fibonacci spiral illustrating the golden mean.

The eight-foot circle within the Artificial Gravity machine has a very tight turning radius, however, which makes it necessary, when trying to run around the edge, to constantly change direction, very much like the Chinese MiG fighter pilots who invented how to contend with smaller turning radii than any pilots had up to that point. Their unpredictable and close-to-impossible turns made them difficult to shoot. According to Fibonacci, a perfect ratio is found in the spiral that travels through the squares and rectangles which pictorially represent the golden mean. Le Corbusier adds, "The bodies of animals and insects also disclose in many of their proportions the theme of the golden section; in the forelegs of the horse, as much as in the index of the human hand, appears the series of three consecutive terms of a diminishing series."[8] It was noticed that there was a common ratio that made things appealing to the eye, 1.6.

This sequence of numbers seems to appear in a wide variety of places in the natural world. Artificial Gravity explores whether there is a perfect radius that would be essential for the human form on a horizontal surface.

So what is the perfect radius for the human run? Say that someone about six feet tall decides to run in a circle as we do *a lot* in "Artificial Gravity." If we examine the difference in effect of running on the perimeter of the eight-foot circle, versus running on the perimeter of the twenty-foot circle, and try to assess what is too much space versus too little versus just enough and why, we might arrive at a standard size for the human dancer to move within. We would arrive at this conclusion through the use of other fields' methods, but might answer a question that has long been left unanswered in our own field: what is the right-sized space for dance to be presented within? Through trial and error, I think there is a discoverable answer. We say four feet is too small because it's impossible to accomplish a true run. With this radius, the run is not functional; its purity and function is compromised. It no longer feels or looks like a run. To perform a human run on a ten-foot radius is about perfect: it is possible within this area to run with power and might and not be left with too much excess unused space. For instance, you could have a radius of a hundred feet, but the human stride would never show itself curving (and generating centripetal force). To a viewer, it would look mostly as if the runner were going in a straight line. The circumstance of a circle would be erased.

This turning disc also generates a constant supply of unexpected angular momentum. The dancer goes from a more stable surface (the still ground) to a moving surface (the disc), and the moment of change creates an uncanny, turbulent force field. I use these unique forces to invent new moves, moves forced into existence from the design of purely physical phenomena. I don't mean metaphysical; I know every single moment a body is on earth is physical. I am speaking about crafting variations away from what we, as human bodies, know as normal. By normal, I mean self-generated volitional motion, which equals meta-movement, as in, yes, you're moving, but not really moving because you don't have to. This "not normal" always refers back to establishing an un-habitual place in space, which eventually is necessary to accomplish a real move!

When dancers get onto the surface of Artificial Gravity, the machine propels them off, and it exerts odd, surprising forces on their bodies. In this particular case, the perimeters of my playing area are circular, the size of the center floor is eight feet across, it spins in two directions, and is mostly never still. The outer six foot-wide, ten-foot-radius floor is also almost never still. It sometimes turns the same direction as the eight-foot center floor, but at different speeds, and at other times turns the opposite direction. Both of these turning surfaces produce unusual and surprising forces. That area is juxtaposed to the ground that does not move (at least not as noticeably as the disc's ground moves). This is mild turbulence; this is constructed uproar. My ideal model of this machine turns at a rate of half a *g*, which is equivalent to half the force of gravity, but it is a gravity force exerted sideways (rather than vertically) on a body. The machine in "Artificial Gravity" moves faster than a treadmill, faster than a ski rope-tow. This machine creates enough energy to enable the dancers to do movements that usually require them to run ten feet, just by standing in place (their place is moving). Their usually necessary props are erased. When you step onto the disc, it is quite abrupt. The initial body response is to push against the turning force. This is an internal isometric impulse, and it works to establish some stability, yet the dancers' vertical position at these moments is at a thirty or sometimes forty-five degree angle. When watching this event, even simple moves seem odd. I will describe a few. Remember, the objective is to create real moves that are in and of themselves not referential or descriptive or emotive. (But they might be metaphoric or emotive as a secondary or tertiary effect.)

MOVE #1: Instructed to walk across the disc in a straight line, two dancers start opposite one another (one upstage, one downstage; one walking toward stage right, one walking toward stage left). Their job is to walk across and pass one another going in opposite directions. This seems simple enough. In fact, it is almost impossible, in the most beautiful way. In rehearsal, we have come to call this moment "the walk of the drunken people." The moment becomes about the odd ground-shift adjustments you have to perform in your body in order to appear to remain in the same space while your ground is moving beneath you (a ground that is not simply passing underneath, but circling). The forces involved are different from mere momentum or mere acceleration (momentum and acceleration have a single thrust to their directionality). When you walk across an eight-foot or twenty-foot turning circle, at every square inch that you advance, the radius becomes a different length (it first decreases and then it increases). The forces change accordingly: at each spot on the radius, the speed of rotation has a different effect on the walking body. That is why there is less turbulence at the center than at the edges. It is surprising that *how* one accomplishes a move often holds the content of that move.

MOVE #2: Another challenge is provoked when I ask all seven dancers to got on the the inner eight-foot circle, balance on its extreme edge in a small second-position paral lel, and lean in at a forty-five degree angle with their arms smeared to their sides. In another instance I ask three dancers to mount the disc at equal distances from one another (which is to say, exactly 120 degrees apart). Their first job is to hold their balance on the outside edge of the inside disc as the turning machine is rotating counterclockwise. They are affixed to the board and, of course, traveling around with it. This is not quite as simple as it sounds, but it's not of the maximum difficulty either. Now I request that they walk backward as if they are Philippe Petit, walking across a tightrope strung between New York's World Trade Towers in 1974. At the same time, I ask them to do this at such a rate that it appears they are remaining in the very same place in space as referenced by the room at large. The question here is how many feet at any one time have to pass under their bodies for them to be successful in essentially NOT leaving their place in space. Another way of stating the question might be this: in order to stay in the same place, how many feet (out of twenty-five feet) have to pass under you, at what speed with each walk or jump, and/or how high must you jump? Can you imagine running like mad, the ground whizzing by in a circular motion below you, and you are not traveling? This relatively recent experiment of having all of my equipment circling was, in part, inspired by a quote I read from the Wright brothers, "When we familiarized ourselves with the operation of the machine in more or less straight flights, we decided to try a complete circle."[10]

Consider another piece of equipment: an eight-foot I-beam weighing about two hundred pounds. An I-beam looks benign enough until you have to decide how long it needs to be (which requires you to cut it). When you cut it, the edges look like blades! The I-beam is attached to a motorized cross truss that travels up and down at will. There is a center attachment and an eye-screw attached to a swivel, which is then attached to a cable that is hooked onto the cross truss. The beam doesn't swing, it just spins around and raises up and down at various distances from the ground. The floor is miked for sound. The beam/blade turns at the motivation of the dancers, and it raises and lowers at the motivation of the motors. As it ominously turns, it goes up and down, sometimes head-high, sometimes just above the thickness of a prone human body. With these movements, the I-beam constructs its own timing parameters. Because its movements affect where in space the dancers can be, it affects timing in a pure and physical manner. You cannot be where the I-beam is. The timing challenge for the dancers is their

"PolarWander," 2009. Photo: Tom Caravaglia.

perception of the beam coming at them or chasing them and exactly how far away it is, therefore, exactly how much time they have to stay where they are. A STREB designation regarding time and space is, "Don't waste either." This action creates a true and real timing system, and an honest occupation and de-occupation of space.

Another machine is called SuperPosition. This piece of hardware is a seven-foot circle whose circumference is a three-feet-wide metal grate, nineteen feet from the ground, and attached to a pivot point at the bottom, which is resting on an axle, and supported by four-angled legs. On the other side of the axle is a very large conical object that helps the circle rotate around a pivot point. Think of the large, yellow structure as a huge, steel snow cone balancing on an axle in between the cone and the circle. When the dancers begin

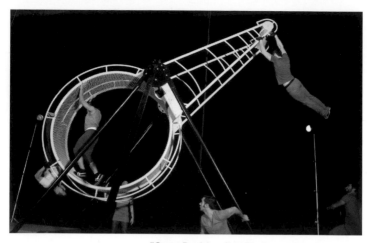

"SuperPosition," 2009. Photo: Tom Caravaglia.

to walk inside the circle on the yellow grate itself, it is an overwhelming experience. You feel the power of slightly twisted space-time just a bit, and the counterweight of the cone hurls through space at your beck and call. Because the counterweight has a different effect at different momentum points on the contraption's rotation, there is a moment of antigravity within the circle. Given the diameter of the circle and the fact that the circle is falling (meaning that the ceiling is lowering) there should not be sufficient space for a body to flip within it. And yet, one of our dancers, Cassandre Joseph, accomplished this.

Noe and Ivan Espana, the inventors and builders of this machine, told me it can go as fast as you can keep up with it, and faster. This is a good definition of the point of no return. You would have about a ton of metal chasing you if you did not keep very close track of what your own velocity limits were at any given time. We spent time running in this machine to test and understand it. I asked if one person could run on the top while another kept running inside, and if this would make it go faster and faster, could the inside body go faster than the outside runner? Then the dancer said, "I think I can get outside the inside of the wheel, while the outside runner dives off the outside and the top." At this very moment, another body jumps back inside the wheel and it keeps on turning. This allows a body to press or "smear" against the inside of the wheel to inscribe a perfect physical circle at nineteen feet above the ground, a space ordinarily impossible to access. Then another dancer gets on the outside by jumping onto the point of the cone as it speeds by the ground. This new outside dancer then does a stomach smear on the outside of the wheel, and as the ground passes, does a banana peel exit, flying off the machine. All of these small, individual moments morph into a possible order, preserving the momentum and rhythmic structure of the gizmo's possibilities and qualities. The last act is to order the events of all the collected physical movements into a brand-new dance. If I try to imagine a body circling like a roller coaster into a full 360 degree circle, it would look and feel like this but be much more complex.

TIME

Even a stopped clock is right twice a day!

I first realized that I wanted to fly when I caught a fly in a mason jar. Wow! I wondered, how do they do that? I fell in a confused love with their erratic and immediate shifts of direction and their untraceable flight trajectories, impossible to memorize. I was jealous. So you see, the origins of my movement interests are pretty grubby. I never dreamt of being a ballerina: I hated the color pink and the fussy, flimsy look of the garments. I found the word "tutu" embarrassing even to say. It all started with a fly, then came my attention to equipment and hardware and things that moved: knobs and gears, even if nonfunctional.

My first choreography in memory premiered one evening in my family kitchen, in front of my parents, who were finishing dinner, reading the newspaper. I noticed that across the room on the countertop was an overfilled box of nuts and bolts, precariously balanced on a stack of magazines. It was very slowly slipping off the shelf. I wandered over slowly, with perfect timing and spatial aim. Swinging around at the very last second, I dropped into a very deep plié and caught the box perfectly horizontally, just an inch from the ground. My measurement of time and space was flawless, and my parents were dumbfounded. There was no applause. They looked up in confusion, then turned back to their reading. But I was changed forever. I knew something significant had happened. It would take about twenty years to figure out exactly what this moment meant.

When I started training as a dancer, I was utterly clueless as to what methods dancers adopted to train their bodies, minds, and hearts to move through space. Looking at myself in a mirror as I moved seemed ludicrous. I knew intuitively that I could do one thing (move) or the other (look in the mirror), but not both. These are mutually exclusive activities. Funny enough, most dance instructors do not know this. They are most interested in the doable parts of dance: how the body looks and its dancer-like positions, otherwise known as technique. This includes the strength, flexibility, facility, articulation, and use of body parts in a particular order.

Dancers learn to dance by counting. What STREB's investigation entails is what happens the very second a body begins to move—this transformative moment when you lose consciousness, when you let the forces conquer you and you barely have your hands on any controls at all. It is then that the mental activity required to gaze out in a particular direction at a wall of mirrors, locate yourself there, and notice what you are doing, not what you are being, becomes patently absurd. At that split second, you discover the difference between thinking and being. This other thing, this letting the bull out of the gate, is what I call a real move. A real move is similar to the time that a bull rider spends on a bull.

The rider must remain on the bull's back through the intense tumult of the bull bucking, twisting, arching, and whirling at immeasurable speeds and in erratic formulas as the bull switches back on itself. With a constantly shifting position, the rider must remain on, with only one gripping hand, to avoid hurtling off into a no man's land of dirt and mighty hooves. These types of movements thicken the air with another type of presence—one that spits in the eye of time and space and slips through both cracks and disappears.

HUNKS OF ACTION

Another principle ballet teachers depend on is the necessity and ubiquitousness of dancing to music. They teach a combination of moves and tell you to count. (A combination in movement is similar to a phrase in music. It's a series of discrete movements hooked together into a continuous, successive, single part. I like to call these "hunks of action.") It all just fell apart for me! I couldn't do it: look in the mirror and now count! I thought, how can I see myself if I'm moving, and how can I move and count simultaneously? I mean *really* move. How can you know the timing of a move before your body does it? This idea seemed backward to me. Here was the age-old mind/body dilemma. I felt intuitively that these two practices were eviscerating movement, the *true* nature of movement. Instructors also request that you not wince or skew your facial muscles; they demand that you keep a relaxed, beautiful look at all times. This perplexed me. When it hurts, I am going to grimace! I thought it logical to represent or let be visible the actual experience of

"BiLevel," The Joyce Theater, NY, 2002.
Photo: Tom Caravaglia.

the degree of physical exertion. I've always wondered why female dancers are always smiling. It is so annoying.

Prior to becoming a modern dance major in college, I was an extreme sports action obsessive. My two specialties were downhill skiing and motorcycle racing. Outside my bedroom window, I would hear the sound of motorcycles progressing through their five gears, and I associated this sound with freedom. (As time went on in my movement career, loud sounds made from machines or human movement registered as dangerous and interesting.) I saved money from working nights as a counter girl in Woolworth's in downtown Rochester, New York, and bought my first motorcycle when I was fifteen. I went through five different bikes over the next seven years. When I graduated to a Honda 350, the biggest one I ever owned, I experimented with exactly how fast I needed to go for the wheels of the machine to lift off of the ground. The answer turned out to be ninety mph. This experiment with such a small bike resulted in a very wobbly and uncertain flight. As Orville Wright said, "It was only a flight of twelve seconds and it was an uncertain, wavy, creeping sort of flight at best; but it was a real flight at last."[1]

At a young age, I started to think of my body as an action machine. I was helping my father on the job—I was his ten-year-old, eighty-pound day laborer. Leonard Streb, a mason by trade, worked long, hard hours laying stone. At one point, he was building a cement foundation up by Lake Ontario, and brought me along. He threw two five-gallon buckets at me and said, "Go fetch some water for me now." I walked down the stony path to the edge of the lake, dipped both buckets in, and started back up the path. Since water weighs about eight pounds a gallon, this was about forty pounds per side, eighty pounds all together. It was extraordinarily heavy, especially for someone my size. This really excited me. I thought, he will not believe I am able to do this, a kid so small and skinny. Here was an experience I had never had before—managing that type of heaviness and difficulty. Every step was a mild impossibility, especially walking uphill on stones. It felt as if the bottom halves of my legs had sunken into the ground, and I was sloughing through dense viscous matter until I got to him and handed the buckets over. He took them, dumped them out, and threw them back at me. I went back down the pathway, got two more, and climbed back up to start again. I was not going to stop until he said, "That's enough." He did just that, five hours later.

What I began to notice early in life was that I was addicted to physicality. I wanted to feel my body pushing, falling, climbing, catching, watching, and crashing with everything and anything that moved. I was already an ecstatic dancer in the world. After accumulating certain memories of motion from these early experiences, I kept waiting to *feel* the move when I started taking dance classes. I kept wondering, when would I sense the intensity I was used to in regards to momentum, velocity, impact, rebound, and weight? I kept waiting to actually *move*. Continually disappointed, I felt as if the fussy little moves were tantamount to telling a lie.

HOW SOON IS NOW

My purpose in this chapter on time is to show that it is the timing of action and the method of execution that holds the key to real movement. Physical forces and the laws of causality take control in the world; they are the rule builders, not us. For example, when a full glass of wine falls from the counter, it just falls straight down and explodes on the ground. It doesn't do three turns on its way down, nor can it choose to pause. A very particular, articulate set of forces are employed by every action, or cause. The "how" of movement is what holds the appeal as an ultimate attention-getter. I was told that the reason it's so hard to compete with the movement of video on a stage is that the timing of video is snakelike—made up of rapid and eccentric motions—and we, as primal animals, succumb to this primitive threat.

Taking time seriously is critical to all movement. In STREB technique, PopAction is about the present tense. It's about now, this moment, this second. But how can we actually define this idea of time which is simply and only the now we are in? This concept is closely aligned with being. Heidegger has a concept of being that he refers to as *Da-sein*: the mode of being that knows it is within time, and particularly knows somehow, that this being in time is framed by the absolute horizon of death. Being is filled with the possibility of "nows"; being acts as a container for the now, and now is all that time can ever be. That is why action and time are inextricable.

Kant had several arguments for his analysis of the a priori existence of space and time; so did Einstein, Bergson,

Newton, Euclid, and more recently, Brian Greene, Michio Kaku, and Lisa Randall. Maybe the point of time is that it isn't a thing in and of itself, but it passes through us, and in our bodies, we feel that something has happened. Thomas De Zengotita, my professor at NYU, told me, "This is too psychological. Kant works with Newtonian time but he thought of it as a category of subjective experience. Time is prior to physicality; time is the passage of experience in our minds.

Happenings are time from the point of view that our experiences of them are time. What, then, causes events to end or to begin or to happen at all? Einstein states: "People like us, who believe in physics, know that the distinction between past, present, and future is only a stubbornly persistent illusion."[2] Perhaps this "arrow of time" habit is caused by our nascent and residual inability to be in the moment. We usually focus on what was, or what will be. This glancing back and forth distracts us from the now. Bergson states: "More generally, in that continuity of becoming which is reality itself, the present moment is constituted by the quasi-instantaneous section affected by our perception in the flowing mass, and this section is precisely that which we call the material world. Our body occupies its centre; it is, in this material world, that part of which we directly feel the flux; in its actual state the actuality of our present lies."[3] We could state that within an extreme movement we notice this "flux," this "being" coursing through our bodies and our minds. We might say, That's it! That's time!—even though the "instant," cannot be captured. Either it hasn't occurred yet or it's already gone.

STREB: Time

REAL TIME

In this examination of time as it relates to movement and the development or discovery of a real move, I want to look into some of the philosophers' thoughts about the nature of time, so that I can borrow at least a modicum of their rigor as I approach this subject myself. I am not a scholar; I am a practitioner, and believe the information I have gathered about time is quite distinct from theirs, yet salient for my purposes. I have been trying to harness the slippery element of time in practical, physical terms, to create an effective movement moment. I may not be able to define precisely what time is, but can I name it, say it, use it deeply? Can I be brave enough and thoughtful enough to embody real time, this side of dying?

In Kant's *Critique of Pure Reason,* he states that space and time are structuring devices or entities, which exist a priori to we humans knowing anything. Time and space are frameworks. They are conditions on the existence of things as we perceive them. They procede knowledge and experience. Some philosophers disagree, but I am with Kant. One can't break down time into smaller, more fundamental parts that end up constituting a subset of the idea of time, after all. A subset of the substance of cement, would be mortar, sand, or water. If you took a part of how we think and experience time, for instance, it would be a minute or a second, each having the exact same materiality as the whole of time.

There are a number of beautiful mathematical and philosophical ways to attempt to align our experience of time and space with reality. John Wheeler writes, "mass grips space by telling it how to curve, space grips mass by telling it how to move."[4] Gottfried Leibniz claimed, "space and time are merely bookkeeping devices for conveniently summarizing relationships between objects and events within the universe."[5] Time does seem to pass, and physical activities, like our heartbeats, occur in sequence, one after the other. It does take time, as we experience or name it, for these events to occur. Would the heart explode if all the heartbeats in one lifetime occurred at once? That would be 2,522,880,000 heartbeats at one time (if you lived to be eighty). Now that would be one great move! At STREB, we have been trying to deduce how short a move needs to be to constitute something a viewer can recognize or perceive as a move. One second? Three seconds? How long does the present tense last?

Time is the container for movement. Everything would freeze if it were not for time; our world would be in complete stasis. It would require *nothing* to be moving, an impossible concept to imagine. In such a world, there would be no cause or effect, only frozen stillness, and there would be no perceiving of this stillness. Maybe things would exist, but maybe they wouldn't. Is there some other access to understanding time, given that it is difficult to define its *thing-ness*? I try to imagine time's nature. Perhaps it is simply, "we are here," and time as it exists is being drawn or pulled through and past us. Defining time also seems to involve discussing movement, and within other philosophical descriptions, movement is made up of thousands of frozen pictures or images, like an Eadweard Muybridge human motion plate.

Kant begins:

In accordance with the testimony of inner sense, changes
are something real. But they are only possible on the as-
sumption of time. Time is, therefore, something real that
belongs to the determinations of things in themselves.
Why, said I to myself, do we not argue in a parallel manner: "Bodies are real, in accordance with the outer senses.
But bodies are possible only under the condition of space.
Space is, therefore, something objective and real which
inheres in the things themselves" . . . Undoubtedly I must
think my own state under the form of time, and the form
of the inner sensibility consequently gives me the appearance of changes.[6]

Norman Kemp Smith further elucidates:

Time is no more than subjectively real . . . Without time
man would indeed exist but not appear. Not his reality
but only his appearance is dependent upon the condition
of time. Man is not, but only appears, when he undergoes
change.[7]

I suppose it would follow that the capacity for change requires movement. If you were to mix time, change, and experience together, wouldn't you end up with movement, or
must movement be called experience? In the end, you can't
conceive of any without the other. They are what Heidegger
calls "equiprimordial."

Kant describes time as a subjective yet a priori phenomenon. In his view, changes reveal the passage of time and
its impact in the same way that space makes bodies real
yet space is clearly more objective—more *graspable*—than

time. Or perhaps this is a human illusion. Actually, Kant wouldn't say that time itself is "graspable," that's either too physical or too psychological. It's more that time "is" the way we grasp experiences subjectively. We see the air in front of us, the empty space that surrounds us, and we name it space. Time is not like this. I can't swing my hand through time, as I imagine I can through space. They are different. My hand's movement happens in time; it moves because of time. Whether it's moving or not, it's in space. Which raises the question of the relationship of time and reality: does reality require time, or does only the *appearance* of reality require time (i.e., for us to notice reality)? Actual experience is congruent to reality. Let's say reality is what absolutely is there and happening, and is not something we imagine is there: a thing, body, or event we can prove empirically beyond our doubt. Time is what your subjective take on experience depends on. It is the sequence of experienced moments. The sequence of experiencing is time.

Let's try this thought experiment: imagine that everything exists that seems to exist (as I gaze out into the world) except for time. Can I distinguish between a human's reality and her appearance? What if I eliminated time from my concept of reality? Would I then appear and disappear? Can I eliminate time from my experience even in my head, and if I can, what is left over, or what is left out? To begin with, if time were not allowed to operate, I guess my heart would stop beating. (It might never have started.) Because a heartbeat requires the one before it and the one after it, it is a linear, durational activity or phenomenon. But the middle heartbeat is the paradox here.

Let's think about it another way. The old-fashioned way information was stored was called the analog system. Vinyl records and cassette tapes used the analog system; iPods and hard drives store information that is digital. To return to my thought experiment: If experience could be digital, would it still require time? If it required just a moment, and in that moment everything happened at once, could it be said to not require time? Does the idea of an instant equal a moment? No, an instant has no duration while a moment has at least some.

Physicists imagine certain events that are outside of time. They imagine imploded singularities, black hole-type events, in which action and matter are entirely absorbed into a sector of space (usually in outer space where the black holes are). This refers to a macro scale of a magnitude so large it's almost impossible to imagine or comprehend. Endless distances can equal infinite space.

It is tempting to imagine that one can infinitely shrink or contract time, but the fact is, a *moment* is not time (at least not in the passage-of-time sense). It is a singular *moment*. What would happen to me, or to action, if it were not allowed to exist within the structured framework of time, as a continuum, like the heartbeat's one, two, three . . . ? Even something happening very rapidly takes time. An explosion that happens in 1/2,000th of a second still takes up time. Speed, therefore, or ultimate brevity, does not help us to imagine non-time.

What if our experience of time were, all of a sudden, to go backward? When you play a video of movement in reverse, with choreography that is constructed close to the ground, it is mystifying that at first viewing it's mostly difficult to discern which way is forward and which way is backward. Thinking about Einstein's theories of time, Paul Davies writes: "Physicists have invented a name for superluminal particles: they are called 'tachyons,' after the Greek word for 'speed.' Roger Clay and his colleagues believed they had found tachyons."[8] These particles go faster than light, or at least approach that speed, and therefore go backward in time. Their existence is not universally agreed upon. The physical test for all theories involving particles that travel close to, or faster, than the speed of light will involve the supercollider in Switzerland. The supercollider is a proton accelerator that produces two protons going in opposite directions that are meant to collide, and then scientists examine the residue. This test will most notably look at the superstring theory, which claims to be the theory that will unify science by connecting relativity theory with quantum mechanics. But that confirmation is not in yet. The other problem with the tachyon is that if we *could* go back in time we could possibly undo our own or someone else's past. Conceptually, tachyons help support Einstein's beautifully stated refutation: the "arrow of time" is truly a stubborn, persistent illusion.

I have tried to imagine a body capable of going so fast it would disappear, or (short of disappearing) at least turn into a blur. When things go very fast, like this bullet through the card, parts disappear. But to disappear is not to leave time; it is more a form of leaving space. In mathematics, a discontinuity is tantamount to skipping a spot in space. What would be the physical explanation for spaces that are unoc-

"Cutting The Card Quickly," 1964. Photo: Harold Edgerton. Minneapolis Institute of Arts, gift of the Harold and Esther Edgerton Family Foundation.

cupiable? Leon Henkin, University of California Professor Emeritus, once posed a similar problem to me: "Can you, as you are falling, skip a spot in space, and then reappear a bit further on, or down?" It's a fascinating idea. Although I have tried, I have not yet solved this physical challenge. I have imagined how it could perhaps be solved but every solution requires a bit of magic and illusion, which is anathema to a true extreme action specialist who believes nothing is impossible.

If Kant is right, and time is not derived from experience but rather precedes experience (as stated in his first argument for the a priori existence of time), then the ineffability of time makes it difficult to imagine its absence. This highlights the inconceivability of the instantaneous moment. As A.C. Ewing mentions in his book on Kant: "It seems also at least plausible to hold that our inability to perceive or imagine these things is not merely a factual but a logical impossibility."[9]

Without abdicating our responsibilities to investigate time and space, let us accept for the sake of practicality that we operate in a classical, Euclidian, Newtonian universe. This journey for me keeps returning to the dialogue between the thinker and the doer, between the scholar and the practitioner. Brian Greene states: "Newton's flawed conceptions of absolute space and absolute time work wonderfully well at the slow speeds and moderate gravity we encounter in daily life, so our senses are under no evolutionary pressure to develop relativistic acumen. Deep awareness and true understanding therefore require that we diligently use our intellect to fill in the gaps left by our senses."[10] This is a definite requirement for choreographers or movement organizers. If time is a unitary (without it there can be no actions, so we cannot afford to take it for granted) and contingent on a section of movement and how it operates, we have a bigger job than I had originally thought. Even if time changes its stripes depending on the size of what we observe—macro or micro, regarding cosmology or particle physics—the study of physics and mathematics is necessary for any choreographer.

RHYTHM

So what trajectory can I, a practitioner, employ to keep the purity, the truth of timing accurate? When inventing actions, how can I be sure not to take the element of time for granted? The law of timing in STREB works like this: you do the move in as much time as it takes your body to do that move (no more, no less) and you do it with your skill set as it exists right now. It is in the repetition of a move, or a series of moves, which are executed embracing the above STREB timing law, that a particular rhythm emerges. In *doing,* we discover that rhythm is a dominant issue in the fundamentals of action. Just as Shakespeare adopted a rhythm that suited his form, dance can acquire its own iambic pentameter based on the fundamentals of move-making. If, on the other hand, movement works only to make images, as Bergson may posit, then rhythm becomes a secondary detail. Audiences leave musicals humming a tune, not having memorized the shape of the singers' lips as they sang. I believe it is absurd to make moves that serve the purpose of freezing positions. Some philosophers believe that movement is just a series of thousands of frozen shapes, but no one particular shape (if you stopped time) holds the essence or nectar of movement.

One day in the late 80s, when I was teaching at the Harvard Summer Dance Program, my musical accompanist became increasingly annoyed with me. He said, "You keep changing the timing of your phrase. With every repetition it's a slightly different rhythm and pace!" I asked him to please explain why that mattered. He said, "It should be uniform so orchestras can stay together!"

"Well, this is clearly not an orchestra. Why else?" He didn't know. I explained to him that each dancer's body is like a slightly different musical instrument. One's a cello, one's a viola, one's a violin . . . We are repeating the hunk of movement over and over, and with each repetition we are letting its true timing be revealed to us, given our increased familiarity with the hunk of movement as well as increased skill. I asked him, "When you walk down the street, do you keep the very same pace in your walk with each passing block? I know one's stride is specific to one's hips and tendons and joints; it's a function of a particular body's mechanics, but beyond that fact, does the body keep exactly the same consistent pace?" He was very annoyed at this point. He said, but that's not the point. But, in movement terms, that is the point. We work on timing with our body as a mechanical unit from the inside out, not the outside in. Eventually, I asked my director, Iris Fanger, to send me only percussionists.

Many scientists have concerned themselves with the notion of the present tense—the now. We can be fairly sure that this now is happening. But how long is now? As with many decisions in the construction of art, one makes a lot of educated guesses using intuition. I believe that two seconds might be the correct amount of time to quantify now. It is quite lengthy in reality, especially in contrast to what Stefan Klein believes—that one-tenth of a single second is the shortest interval in which a human is capable of taking in or noticing an event.[11]

Given the difficulty of prompting an audience member to pay attention to a critical moment in a dance, or any particular moment for that matter, I'd say that if that moment only lasted one-tenth of a second, most of the audience would miss it (or not believe their eyes). In a performance, set-up and recovery time is necessary, if not for the movers or for the rhythm of the movement, then in order to point to the moment effectively on which you are trying to focus the viewer's attention. That critical moment, or middle second (the one we are pointing to), typically ends up being ten times longer than I believe it needs to be in order for it to be noticed. But the extra, surrounding moments increase the chances that the audience will, in fact, notice what I'm trying to present to them. If my experiments in the studio hold true, humans need many moments to notice a single now. To put it another way, what we have found is that even if there can be said to be a singular event called now, that now has to have duration if it is to be noticed (at least by humans).

THE TEN-SECOND DANCE

Recently, we began setting a challenge to invent what we call ten-second dances. This is based on a growing suspicion that movement might be, by its nature, episodic and not durational. Could it be that an essential action such as sliding, falling, spinning, rebounding, wiggling, or writhing, could constitute and contain as much content as a forty-minute dance, if framed and presented clearly enough?

Kant's third argument for the a priori existence of time includes his commentary on the difference between successive and simultaneous.[12] These are beautiful concepts to

"Artificial Gravity," 2009. Photo: Tom Caravaglia.

use in an effort to investigate the two distinct yet connected realities of space and time. What STREB tries to do is to densify the air with action. Because of forces such as gravity (the weakest of the four forces), it is difficult to put one body under another or two or three in the air at the same exact time. Imagine one diving two inches from the ground while another is flipping back over that same diver, both of these bodies going in opposite directions, and yet another dancer diving downstage between the two. This movement assembly, lasting two seconds, is categorically STREB. It requires the use of timing devices that only we employ. (Most other extreme action specialists, like gymnasts, are mainly soloists. Circus tumblers might come closest.) The specific type of milli-inch and millisecond activity STREB has developed is, I believe, the closest you can get to the digital live-time storage of action events. I often say that if I could perfect this and let *all* movement happen at once, my entire show would be three seconds long.

STREB work is quintessentially about *now*. It is what we call a present tense technique in which we attempt to honor this moment, given it's all we have access to. We accept the functional truth of this. Henri Bergson's idea of real duration describes how we, in the present moment, sense or experience the idea of time as a phenomenon. Bergson held that we do not need to utilize the act of spatializing the nature of this experience (which in essence would be to measure it). He also suggests that to do so would be a categorical misnomer, since time operates independently of space:

> To measure duration, then, is to translate indivisibility into instants, conceived as points on a line which we take in at one glance. Real duration is directly intuitional; the translation into static space is useful for some purposes but it is not the original experience—just as the translation of a poem does not claim to be the poet's original creation. This duration of the original experience we directly intuit but cannot conceptualize; it is part of us; it is integral to our experience and to the aspects of the world which appear in that experience. It is the reality within which we dwell.[13]

In other words, time is indivisible unless you choose to artificialize it by measuring or dividing it.

Time does seem to be the refuge of movement. Given that both are invisible yet present (if not as objects then certainly as experiences), there's all the more reason for us to examine how an audience perceives and/or experiences time and movement. I don't think most dance is staged

"Gauntlet x 3," 2009.
Photo: Tom Caravaglia.

effectively, nor has it been deeply examined. When looking at conventional dance presentations, Heather Carson, a great visual and lighting artist whom I worked with for eighteen years, asked me, "Where do the dancers think they are going when they disappear into the wings? And where do they think they are coming from when they reappear?" I have not yet heard a reliable answer to this question from any choreographer. I see this as a deep problem in the field at large along with all the other unanswered questions.

Time has never held a building together. Nuts and bolts and concrete and steel have. Why, then, would we expect an aural structure (like music) to be used as a compositional tool for something essentially physical, like movement? Structure for physical issues needs to be physical. That is why I believe music is the true enemy of dance. I don't believe anyone has analyzed the temporal structure of movement yet, or developed a nomenclature or lexicon for the specific rhythms made by the actions of the human body. Perhaps this lack of a naming process, or a named knowledge base in movement, is why people tend not to remember the movement they have witnessed.

In my work as a choreographer who constructs extreme action events for live-time situations, I have noticed that humans don't like to go very fast, especially if it hurts. (Going really fast hurts mostly because of the utilization of force, which needs to erupt from the increased bend in the ankle and the knee, at least in the vertical plane of space.) In initiating movement, a body edges up against the constraint of its own weight and contends with the havoc caused by gravity in a time-based system. Having to execute action in a gravity-laden world, in live time, causes the body to encounter a wall of another interesting, rather foreign sensation. (Remember, we at STREB don't use the word "pain.") The normal, everyday body responds to this by taking it easy. Usually taking it easy means slowing down. If a dancer or action specialist concedes to the ineffability of time, or doesn't analyze it rigorously, it's as dangerous as ignoring the nature of space. You risk creating a murky series of movements, or you risk not meaning what you do. Moreover, you risk never achieving the presentation of a real move. Actually, I am not sure this is possible for the human to achieve without dying. But we can edge up real close to that line of no return.

INVISIBLE FORCES

So the challenge becomes how to contend with time. In my view, movement events follow (or need to follow) a very different temporal structure than aural ones (i.e., music events). The timing or pacing of movement events depends on entirely different factors: the mechanical measurement of the legs, arms, torso, neck, hips, feet, shoulders, ankles, and knees; the alchemetic processes of the neurological systems of the human being; the size of your heart; your lung capacity; the flexibility of your tendons, ligaments, and muscles; the size of your quads, glutes, and calves and their capacity for growth. These factors play a big role in determining not just how long a particular human being takes to move through space, but in what manner as well. So with different bodies, dynamics are dramatically distinct. The "how" includes issues of grace, power, and other particulars, such as choice of accents, and decisions of how much or how little force to apply. Often, the physical and technical practice for dance will involve doing pliés, stretches, and calesthenic exercises along with low-impact training and muscle building. These exercises serve a purpose: they increase the range, speed, and accuracy of the body that chooses to move. You have to get the muscles onto the correct spot on your skeleton so there is no motion impeded by a muscle mass. Your joints become fully free. When the human machine is required to fly or fall from high edges, then, like a NASCAR car, every part of the dancer's machine has to be honed to become a generous and expeditious moving device.

If the most efficient amount of time needed for a particular human to execute a particular move is equal to x, then the perfect execution of the event is always equal to x. Therefore our goal is to be honest and accurate about these moves in time with each and every action, and to understand their true timing-length. This true timing should only be ascertained after a high level of skill is achieved. Movement doesn't lie, yet people could, if not careful, force the timing of certain moves and in so doing, misrepresent what the system of movement might truly be. When the timing of a movement is forced, it artificializes the move and the moment. I have noticed that timing is *the* critical factor in the shaping of effect. You might be listening to the most brilliant and fascinating intellectual in the world revealing to you the map of the holy grail, and some erratic physical act or accident, like a banana peel slip, happens an inch

away, you will automatically, I mean *immediately,* take your attention towards the action, towards the movement. You will not be able to focus on the most crucial event of your life. *Whammo,* you are gone; your attention is held captive by your passion for rubbernecking.

Is there ever a concrete aspect to time, and can it ever be captured? Can time be not just measured, but also *seen*? Does time have an artificial signifier? Perhaps the closest we come to keeping time is on clocks. Looking at a clock, one can almost see time go by, with the second hand turning round and round on the clock face. But there is really no such thing as keeping time. Clocks and other time-measuring devices are used to prevent train crashes and to order events. But what is time's signifier, apart from the clock? What is a time-keeping shape or a time-keeping

"Gauntlet," 2009. Photo: Tom Caravaglia.

movement? Could it be the pendulum swing? Is the pendulum the very real shape of time keeping itself? Can I design something, an event, that tells true physical time? These questions became the basis for a STREB production called "STREB Brave."

The hardware and equipment in STREB are used to assist us in getting to new, un-habitual places in space. Could one piece of equipment create a situation that mirrors time and not space? Is there a more quintessential time-keeping shape than the pendulum? The pendulum is a tracer, a perpetual engraver, the bottom edge of a circle. I suspected that the arc could qualify to be such a shape. One of the challenges in developing this piece was whether I would be able to capture or design something that could tell "true" physical time, or at least signal that information. Would that be a classic shape that would obey nature's temporal laws—a non-arbitrary, lateral arc or curve, for example? Would that be it?

In 2004, I was commissioned by Jazz at Lincoln Center to stage a performance. I hung a ninety-pound cement block on a twenty-foot cable so that it rested just nine inches off the floor. This piece was called "Gauntlet." Our stage area had been established as twenty-by-twenty feet, the necessary amount of space for action. When the block was pulled out to the side of the space and released, first it swung at the entire twenty-foot span of the playing area, then slowly, incrementally, its arc shrank. Magically, it took exactly the same amount of time to complete whichever sized arc it eventually corrupted to, until (after a surprisingly long time) the block came to stillness.

This primitive machine posed a spatial problem as well as a temporal one. Before I began to create this dance, I experimented with using three or four different cement blocks at slightly different heights, therefore different radii. In the end, I settled on two cement blocks exactly upstage/downstage from one another, and two average body widths apart from one another. The only difference was that the upstage block was twenty inches from the ground, while the downstage block rested at nine inches. When the downstage block was under its direct hang-point, a foot, an ankle, an arm could safely fit underneath it. A head, a torso, or a butt could not. Upstage, the entire body (lying down) could pass under the block, wherever it was in its swing. The two cement blocks had slightly different temporal periods, as manifested in the full-to-still swing of their arcs. The point is, the dance was built temporally first and spatially second, exactly the opposite of what I ordinarily do. The timing system for the blocks was the most essential issue. If you understood that system, there was only one place in space (and only one instant in time) to either be or not be—but only for a moment before the block came swinging back, and that was patently obvious!

However, it is the exact measurement of space and time in this set of conditions that remains lightly speculative. This is the type of speculation in STREB work that is not desirable. At a performance in Palo Alto, California, I overheard a high school student speaking coolly to his cohorts: "Those are Styrofoam blocks; they're not real!" I thought about doing this; it would have made the entire process of making this piece more reasonable. But the fact of the matter is, a fake block would not move the same as a ninety-pounder. That is perhaps why, gleaning from the gasp-like sounds from the rest of the audience, most people could tell it was real.

MOTION

There is an art . . . a knack to flying.
The knack lies in learning how to throw
yourself at the ground and miss.
—DOUGLAS ADAMS

As a kid, I often sat down with my mother, Carolyn Elliot Gale (Streb), for serious conferences concerning what I should "do" with my life. My mother, having rescued me from an orphanage at the age of two, was my soul partner, my savior. She was a powerful example of ethical brilliance. She never lied, or put on airs, or gossiped. In my experience, she was never unkind. She laughed heartily at events that tickled her. She helped me notice small occurrences that most people ignored, such as the wind, the waves, small unsuspecting bugs that acted oddly, certain colors, birds, and very old trees. "Oh, Bet!" she'd exclaim "Look! How glorious!" In these moments, she always used slightly old-fashioned exclamations.

My mother took my life inquiries very seriously, putting aside time to confab with me. She would look me straight in the eyes as we tried ardently to figure something out. She respected and supported my ideas. When I announced my desire to become an artist, she drove me to the Rochester Memorial Art Gallery every week so that I could study drawing and painting. She did this consistently from the

time I was eight through thirteen. We discussed other ideas of what might be of interest and hold potential for my future. We came to hasty decisions—tennis, hunting, fishing, speed skating, waterskiing, bowling, basketball, baseball! Each time, she would buy me all the necessary accoutrements for each activity. So in 1959, when I turned nine years old, I asked for a pair of skis for Christmas. I must have seen someone doing it on TV; there was absolutely no one that I knew who skied. Working-class kids in the 60s did not take up snowskiing. On Christmas afternoon, I begged my mother to take me to Ellison Park Hill. Initially, strapping two sticks onto the bottoms of my feet seemed nuts. But I thought the locking devices that kept ski boots on the wooden platforms were beautiful. The fact that the surface area of the body part which adhered a person to the ground increased by at least a sixfold expansion of the sole of the

RIGHT: **ES with new snow skis, 1963.**
OPPOSITE: **ES in snowshoes with dog, Suzie, 1958.**

foot, piqued my curiosity. This artificial growth of the foot's sole allowed more contact, and so in concert with snow, there was an extreme rate increase. Clearly a person could go faster in these circumstances.

I learned a lot from skiing. One of the rubrics of STREB technique is to remove all transitions so that only the move is happening; nothing is volitional or artificial. This means you need to eliminate all preparations and all recoveries, designating them unnecessary. Whizzing downhill on skis is a perfect exercise of this principle—it's *all* moves. There is a natural force field intersecting every second: you can't fake it if you try.

Ellison Park Hill was perhaps a couple hundred feet long. There was no chair lift or even a rope tow. You'd get to the bottom somehow, take your skis off, walk back up, put them on, and go down again. With no training, my initial descents were abrupt and brutal, even for such a short distance. I didn't understand that all the techniques in skiing are essentially designed to control speed. I would head straight down in an egg position (which, twenty years later, became the "ball" or "clump" of PopAction). Wow! What a feeling! To be completely out of control! As I whipped straight downhill, the other skiers stared in disbelief at what a fool I was.

I thought snowskiing would be similar to waterskiing, where you laterally weight one water ski more than the other, then lean out over that ski and presto, you turn. Snow turned out not to be at all like water. The earth did not move under me when I pressed into it, favoring one ski.

I didn't think the falls were so bad, not like falling on ice. You're already falling anyway. Of all the physical exploits I had tried up to this point, skiing stood out. Even to an untrained mind, the motion of it felt different from the motion of tennis, say, or basketball. It was more urgent, all-engaging. All about now! It hurtled your entire body through space, not a limb here and there. I encountered the phenomenon of speed in a new way, and eventually, the idea of controlling the turn. Turning is the technical raison d'être for the ski's edge. The edge of the ski is basically the device necessary to *not* reach the point of no return on your trajectory downhill, what is also called terminal velocity. There's a speed beyond which it's too fast to stop. I sensed at a young age that this idea of going fast, and at the same time trying to turn, would lead to a valuable set of experiences.

Much later, I learned that the philosopher Heidegger distinguished between different categories of now. He mused that "our external world is actually ordered by the fundamental principles of Space and Time, but our inner world, the world of experience, or sense, or phenomenological noticements, is noticed temporally, not spatially."[1] What might Heidegger think about snowskiing? He would probably agree that its time category is of the "making-present" sort. Making-present is above all the conditions that make it possible for such a thing as now, as in *now this* or *now that*, to be expressed. Heidegger's notion of time is the difference between the past or what he calls "thrownness" and the future, which he calls "possibility." What is in between those two things is what he calls the "making present" or the now, in the sense that "something is manifesting."

Somehow, extreme physical experiences of this sort are in themselves pure, complete, truly existential. Both time and space are exaggerated, or at least in experiential terms, they are difficult to ignore. Heading downhill fast insists on happening in space; time is there as well, but the "where" of it seems all-important. Our perceptions seem to drift to pure sensation, as our stomachs feel lifted into our throats, and the wind becomes a coating all over our bodies. Forces like momentum and acceleration, once quite abstract, reach concrete noun-like status. Directionality is down and the nature of the hill demands this. Skiers use the term fall line for this idea. Straight downhill is the domain of expert skiers because they know how to resolve the problem of reaching seventy mph on the slopes. The properties of a snow-covered hill are unique: slick, thick, cold, icy (the last certainly applies to the East Coast). These properties allow the achievement of certain movements, once the bottoms of the skis meet the surface of the slope. The notion of adding devices to physical conditions, and inventing hardware to accomplish new goals, would recur for me as I began to apprehend that these innovations are a necessary step toward our achievement of a real move. These artificial mechanical amendments are also necessary for getting into other sorts of un-habitual places in space where amazing new forces can be generated.

In STREB work, we don't decide on our timing until all the other facts of action have been attended to. This is in contrast to most choreography, which makes that decision first, and usually in adherence to a soundtrack of sorts. As I have noted earlier, if you adhere to musical timing first, you more or less ignore causality, and no true movement conditions ever result.

FIGHT OR FLIGHT

Action exists at the invisible nexus of time, forces, motion, and body. These four doorways are the portals through which action passes and becomes itself. None of the four is touchable, yet they are the true heartbeat of life itself. How, then, do I deal in a *real* way with such a slippery subject? Action can take your attention away from the most engaging dialogue. Motion is a signifier of life itself, the single most dominant form, the insistent determinant of human intent, function, and uselessness. Action precedes sound, for heaven's sake! It begins with the heartbeat. The motion I am talking about is irreducibly human and animal. When we warily glance at strangers on the street, we are seeking to assess if a stranger will do us harm; we search for physical signals in the way they move. We have an animal instinct known to anthropologists as the fight-or-flight reflex. It is perhaps less useful than it was to us thousands of years ago, but we still persist in participating in the act that could save us. It boils down to noticing actions—the actions of animate and even inanimate objects (cars veering off the roadway, for instance). What secret we seem to understand instinctively is that hidden movements have a predictive moment if we pay close attention to them.

As choreographers, this domain is our treasure trove. We are claiming this territory of content, the meaning encased in motion, actions, gestures, glances, erratic movements, and all that is stored in the rhythm of pure locomotion. We are the storers of action-thoughts and are trying to assemble these moments into some archetypal nomenclature of agreed-upon meaning. But in order to establish these rubrics (governing actions), we must plot a system of discovering real moves and implementing them. Our job, as the finders and manufacturers of action-based moments, is first, as stated earlier, to establish the true rhythmic structure of movement. In other words, if all the structural rules inherent in movement discovery are followed, these moves will have true content of the sort only action produces.

I could sum up STREB methodology as inquiry into that which is unquestionably true, unnoticeable, and absurd. Here are methods we impose in the studio: incorporate and harness invisible forces; let your face make any expression it feels, especially reflecting the physical experience you are now having; get off your feet to change your base of support; develop impact technique; take the hit; question the hegemony of the floor; make action episodic and abrupt not durational and smooth; name a move you are unwilling to do; name an impossible move and do it; create real turbulence; eliminate transitions; ask what is the content of action, then answer it; go and remain outside your comfort zone; break the fourth wall with substance; abandon a skeletal method for initiating movement; develop a nomenclature for action rhythms; occupy vertical space; occupy vertical surfaces; develop human flight; show the effect of action on substance, i.e., dive through glass; do not camouflage the impact of gravity; stop being careful; agree to get hurt; invite danger; defy transitions; explode.

These inquiries lead us to make certain Newtonian demands: develop a nomenclature for action rhythms and felt timing systems; timing is emergent, not a decision; nounize action instead of the body; reimagine the design of action rooms; ask how high you can fall from; believe in human flight; pop the muscles; redefine grace for action; investigate the iambic pentameter for movement; know that music is the true enemy of dance; rob the floor of its hegemony; isolate the direction of up; have more than one body in same space at the same time; occupy un-habitual places in space; get out of cliché-ridden spaces; be out of control when moving; make action the subject, not the body; fly.

The absurdist inquiries alone will keep me busy for the next twenty years. They include: never land; continue to fall; skip a spot in space; try leaving the room through the

STAND

1. ELEPHANT STANDS OFF STAGE FACING FOUR STANDING BODIES

#1

2. AS E WALKS ON STAGE, 4 BODIES FALL BACKWARDS BETWEEN THEM + in A SINGLE E WALKS MOVE - PUTS ONE FOOT ON EACH BODY.

"Stand" drawing by ES, 1999. The idea is for an elephant dance where the elephant would stand on four people, one foot each. The subject is weight.

wall; question that we have to choose a single direction to move in at any one time; represent distinct size on stage and change it and have this change noticed; represent distinct distance on stage; change one's usual rate to rapid; be on fire; create a new substance that moves like none other; move in an unrecognizable fashion; make moves that go noticeably backward; corrupt the effect of the "arrow of time"; create a non-cause-and-effect moment; invent a mistake; stage turbulence; disintegrate order; make the verb a noun; let an elephant stand on you; get hurled by a powerful machine; reach terminal velocity on stage; stop always stopping; move in the same way that bits of Styrofoam twirl in the wind (exactly); create single essential acts (quiver, writhe, shake, wiggle, flail, squirm); go so fast that the glass doesn't break; move so fast you stand still; defy reason; disappear; make a list of moves you will never do again because they are so untrue and embarrassing.

When you take just one aspect of one of these challenges from the above list, you realize how subtle these ideas can be. How do you isolate one of those maxims and develop a clear methodology to examine it? These attempts can produce surprising outcomes that could create rich movement ideas. Think about the concept of grace as it relates to motion (as opposed to sound or painting or literature)—it's all about transitions. When does a moment shift to the next moment? If quintessential grace is tantamount to having no transitions, then how do you get from one movement to the next?

SYNTAX OF MOVEMENT

In the chapter on space, I discussed what constitutes the true occupation of physical space. I tried to describe, using STREB principles, what it might take, physically and temporally, to enact a real move. In the body chapter, I outlined the way the body might enter into these spatial regions and survive. We are concerned not only with certain spatial and temporal operatives, but also with the need to regard the forces embedded and manufactured in these invisible zones. What remains now is to argue why action must be extreme in order for witnesses to notice it, to see it as real movement.

First, it must have rhythm, which I believe is the content of real action. Content is not the same as meaning. Meaning is conferred on movement by outside observers, perhaps academic analysts, perhaps dance critics. But such meaning depends on a syntax and a grammar that movement does not inherently possess. What could be the grammar, the syntax of movement? The well-known linguistic dictum that a sentence can be formed by combining *any* noun phrase with *any* verb phrase was called into question by Noam Chomsky's famous phrase: "Colorless green ideas sleep furiously." I wonder, what are the necessary and sufficient combinations that constitute meaning in movement? It is not that just any order creates deep and distilled movement meaning. The rules for music certainly cannot create coherent meaning for action. My sense is that the key to these questions is rhythm.

So continue to ponder how to assiduously consider the idea of motion. What is it? You can't see it, it's not there yet, or it's already gone, and in the absolute second of the now, it appears to reside in that object that does it, or performs it, the body. But that can't be right, the body is the body. It's not what it's doing; it has to be what is happening to it. Bergson states:

> We generally say that a movement takes place in space, and when we assert that motion is homogeneous and divisible, it is of the space traversed that we are thinking, as if it were interchangeable with the motion itself. Now, if we reflect further, we shall see that the successive positions of the moving body really do occupy space, but that the process by which it passes from one position to

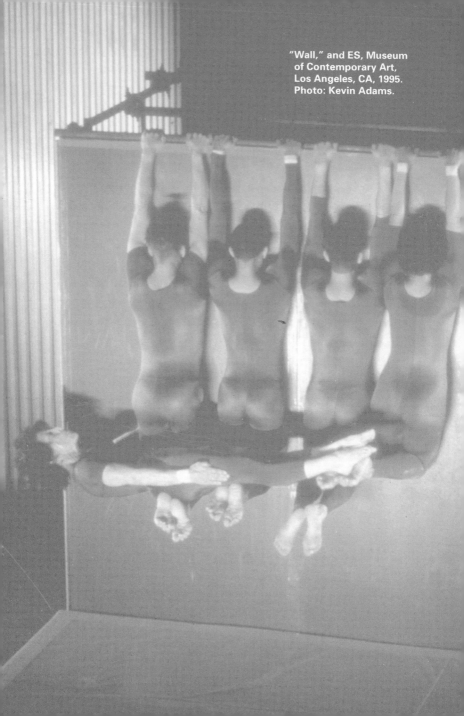

"Wall," and ES, Museum
of Contemporary Art,
Los Angeles, CA, 1995.
Photo: Kevin Adams.

the other, a process which occupies duration and which has no reality except for a conscious spectator, eludes space.[2]

This statement lends itself to thinking about the ineffable quality of movement, and the fact that it can't be seen. To say it's visible is referring only to what Bergson notes as positions that are forever changing.

I believe Bergson considered motion as a series of stroboscopic frozen images very much like the work of photographers Eadweard Muybridge, Étienne-Jules Marey, or Harold Eugeno Edgerton. He sees the element of time manifested within or between each of these radiating images of, in this instance, the horse galloping. He even says: "Of the gallop of a horse our eye perceives chiefly a characteristic, essential or rather schematic attitude, a form that appears to radiate over a whole period and so fill up a time of gallop. It is this attitude that sculpture has fixed on the frieze of the Parthenon."[3] This is a beautiful idea of the consideration of motion, but it leaves out the most confusing parts that have to do with force, and initiation of movement, and all that disappears after a move is over, once the horse stops moving. People watching a horse run seem to have a habit of saying "the horse is galloping" rather than "there is gallop." The verb, therefore, is dragged into the noun-like category, for comfort's sake. This is my complaint with dancing—the emphasis is often on the body and not on the motion.

I am reminded now of my early choreographic years. I was deeply influenced by Muybridge. I bought all of his books I could find on human and animal motion in order to study what happens to us, to humans, when we execute an action. In my observation and study of these beautiful plates of action, I concluded that humans make an enormous number of unnecessary movements. I thought surely I can eliminate some of these perhaps useless and time-consuming preparatory moves and just do it: jump, flip, fly, or fall. Muybridge's plates illustrated this fact: plates and plates of running before you get to the juicy part—the jump! Looking through Muybridge's books over and over, I extracted the critical parts of the movement moments, the subjects. In my own work, I wanted to cut out most of the preparatory and recovery movements. I wanted to do just the move. If I could do this successfully, I would be left with the nugget—the jump, the run, the leap, the fall, the punch. How to accomplish this physically is a larger problem.

I learned that photographers like Muybridge achieved what they did with the photography of actions by inventing new techniques or equipment. It would start with a crazy idea—to stop the motion of a bullet or a horse or a hummingbird. These were impossible dreams: to create pictures that could capture fast actions in a frame. They would just turn out blurry. Everyone knew that! Muybridge used the wet plate process, a relatively slow method of photography. The resulting images were hardly more than silhouettes, but they showed what had never before been seen by the unaided eye. He was commissioned by Leland Stanford in 1872 to discover whether or not, when a horse is galloping, all of his feet are off the ground. He eventually discovered, as we all now know, that they are!

STREB: Motion

THE MOVEICAL

One way to recognize a real move might be to consider whether, at a given point in time, a mover could choose to be still. (If you are not really moving, you are certainly not performing a real move.) For instance, unless both feet are off the ground you're not really moving because you don't have to: there's no emergency situation at hand (such as figuring out how to land); there's no urgency. If the mover can physically choose to stop moving mid-move, the move in question is not real. Real movement is when you have no access to volitional stasis; you are not able to choose to stop.

However, this particular marker can lead one to make false judgments. For instance, just because a person is not doing anything, it doesn't follow that that person can be said to be truly still. Take the example of a falling body. Such a body is moving (because of gravity), and yet, viewed against the backdrop of no-context (no frame) it could appear to be still. To itself, it might even appear still. Einstein said, "If a person falls freely he will not feel his own weight."[4] This means that a falling body might perceive itself to be still or unmoving. Just because a body is not doing anything, does not necessarily mean a body is not moving. In the case of a falling body, I believe a real move is happening, regardless of the will or even awareness of the mover. A person falling cannot stop his or her descent—only the ground or an intervening object like a bungee cord can do that. If you, the viewer, were moving alongside the mover in perfect parallel (and without acceleration), you would not *feel* as if you were moving, and the other falling body might well appear still.

So as I have stated previously, a real move is a move you get hurt trying to stop. That perhaps is the clearest way to define it. Think about the swaying of leaves on trees, or the branches of trees themselves. I couldn't argue that they are not moving, but I call that kind of movement a meta-movement more than a real move. A tree that crashes down during a lightning storm—that's a real move. You'd certainly get hurt trying to stop it.

Why does any of this matter? It's my belief that if a "moveical"—a theatrical action or movement show, where action itself is the subject—is ever to be as profound and substantive as a drama, symphony, or musical sometimes is, it must be composed of real movements. The effect on an audience of such a real movement event would be felt first in the body and only later (much later) in the mind. The gut is faster than the brain or the eyes. I am positing that dance, or movement art, has until now ignored the possibility that the body alone might be the route to a great theatrical moment.

Recently, I met Karla Galdamez, a PhD candidate in physics, who claimed: "It is my belief that that which can be known through mind can also be known through body and vice versa. Since we are an integrated system of body and mind, this connection must exist. It is likely that your suggestion as to the 'lack of a language' that describes the dance experience makes it nearly impossible to speak of that which is known through dance. Maybe if such language developed, one could begin to point at the experiences of the individual in both fields. I am fully emerged in the physics aspect of knowing through the mind. I would be glad to collaborate in understanding the physics in exchange for understanding the movement."

There is much work to do. In movement-invention terms, I have spent more than twenty-five years asking Newtonian and Euclidian questions about action (the sort of action governed by the physical explanations described by these two giants of science). After all, Newton's and Euclid's laws are what we have to deal with here on earth. Even though I might far rather defy Newton's laws, I can't avoid them. My dancers and I have to agree to get hurt trying to defy them, at the very least.

More recent theories of physics deal with infinitesimally small and wildly large issues like particles, strings, or waves traveling at the speed (or close to the speed) of light (186,000 miles per second and 671,000,000 miles per hour), juxtaposed with outer space, and enormous distances mirroring occurrences which transpired millions and millions of years ago; in short, examining mammoth time periods and searching for traces of activities from long ago. To accomplish these measurements, they are literally gazing at the light of stars that is just reaching us over vast distances, the light which shone literally billions of light years ago. If superstring theorists such as Brian Greene are correct, there are at least six hidden extra dimensions that may affect us (aside from the three we know, plus time). But those extra dimensions are tightly bound up together and therefore hard to notice. They apply to particles a billion billion billionth the size of an atomic nucleus. It is hard to make a dance about them or use their rule structures, at least those we know of now.

A turning body on a turning wheel, 2010. Photo: Tom Caravaglia.

When I look at the conditions I have designed to get a body into a domain with un-habitual parameters, it seems to me that the physical challenge that remains is to connect two unlikely or seemingly impossible moments. For instance, one STREB move has a body horizontally in the air spinning three feet above the ground, similar to a helicopter blade. Can I rush the body into an "around the world" flip (another STREB move in which a dancer launches herself from her feet directly backward into a 360 degree rotation and lands on her stomach), but landing ten feet higher up and stopping there, mid-air? Obviously, I would have to figure out how to defy gravity and a few other challenges before I could complete such a move. If I *was* able to do this (or come close to executing this move), we could then repeat it over and over and quite possibly reveal a rhythm for the new moment. All physical rhythms emerge in this way. Consider Cecchetti ballet as opposed to the Russian ballet system, which is more stylized and less functional as a technical training. Both the Russian and Italian systems are about the execution of the ballet idiom, but the execution of the movements, rhythms, and style is radically different. In the Cecchetti method, there is nothing haphazard about the system, nothing which depends on the teacher's mood of the moment. There is a definite plan to daily classes.

A Manual of Theory and Practice of Classical Theatrical Dancing from the Cecchetti method is an excellent source of information on technique, stance, positions of arms, feet, legs, hands, body, head, port de bras, adages, etc. Margaret Craske and Friderica Derra de Moroda later collaborated with Cyril Beaumont in recording many allegro enchainements and pirouettes. I was taught for a year and a half by Margaret Craske, and then by Diana Byer, a student of hers. The specificity of the training was remarkable. There was only one exact rhythmic way to execute the exercise called a dégagé (a technical exercise for the foot to train for petite allegro, fast footwork found in the ballet vernacular), or a téndu (a technical exercise for the foot, done on a different part of the rhythm than the dégagé, and intended to train the body for grand allegro, large traveling jumps). The beauty of Cecchetti's method is its functionality.

This very classical methodology for ballet helps to frame my beef with modern dance, with its physical and formal carelessness. Every movement tells its own motion story, but only if it's based in some manner in a causal reality. This is because causality rules physicality (when we deal with words, we use rules of grammar to communicate). In the Cecchetti method, the difference in rhythm between a téndu and a dégagé is drilled into you over and over again because they are meant as training devices for the execution of different actions. They are a means to an end. The téndu is on the "and one" count: when you feel the "one" you strongly close your heel into first (or another) position against the other heel and it snaps back out again to a téndu stretch. This training of the téndu is rhythmically specific: it was designed to train the body for big jumps or grand allegro. By the same token the dégagé, which emphasized a different part of the count for its rhythm, was geared for petit allegro. A great teacher such as Margaret Craske, or Diana Byer, could tell without looking, just by the sound, if your technique was correct.

The experiment continues. I think the language of movement is located not merely in abstract invention. It is located everywhere on earth. I collect these archetypal types of action by gazing at how people, things, and animals move. There is more information in the world than in my studio. I sometimes think of myself as a motion anthropologist. I collect moves that people do because they must, or just because they do. Both of these kinds of movements possess a quality of inevitability.

I believe motion and motion events can be powerful signifiers, and when accurate enough, can operate as an allegory to remind people of experiences they have had or those they remember happening to others. These holy moves have been encrypted into the bodies of every human, no matter how rich or poor, active or passive. Maybe these archetypes function like smells. Like the smell of cut grass in early spring or your mother's perfume or pine needles around the holidays. I am continually searching for these moments in time and space and body.

THE REAL MOVE

**Last time I saw movement like that,
someone yelled grenade!**
—MAINTENANCE WORKER, VIRGINIA MUSEUM OF ART

In June 1997, I agreed to dive through glass at The Joyce Theater in New York City, at a gala event honoring Cynthia Gehrig, the President of the Jerome Foundation in St. Paul, Minnesota. Cynthia had been a pivotal support in my early years of choreography, and I wanted to do something special to honor her and The Joyce. The Joyce Theater, the only purely dance theater in the country, was a vital supporter of the presentation and realization of my work for many years. I was practicing over the week before the event while vacationing in Jamaica, with my partner Laura.

I was focused on the distances. Distance, in STREB choreography, has to be exact. But estimations are all we have access to! I knew I had only three steps, three very long power run steps, before arriving at the place where I had to punch-dive in order to get through the pane of framed glass my technical director had constructed for me. The bottom of the frame was three feet from the floor; the size of the glass pane itself was a two-and-a-half-foot square. There were many miniscule techniques involved in the perfect execution of the dive. I had to hit, punch, then in a nanosecond drive my heels up to hip level as I horizontally dove through the glass dead center, otherwise I would hit the frame. The power run had to generate enough force to allow me to fly through the air and through the frame horizontally, remaining at that already established latitude line, and exactly (at least) the length of my body with my arms stretched overhead, arms leading with my fists. Speed was necessary as well to get through and beyond the glass. I had to do a perfect line drive, then punch a hole in the glass as big as the circumference of the largest part of my body. My largest parts are my shoulders and my hips. The glass was hanging from two cables, one at each of the top two corners of the frame. The punch had to be a rapid-fire ricochet punch, so that when the glass exploded, the hanging frame would not swing. If the frame moved with me, I would fail. You don't want it swinging. The hit needs to be dead center, otherwise you'll cut yourself on the edges of the glass, separate from the hole you punched, or you'll fall on them; thus, fail. I could not let that happen.

I had rehearsed for this two-second dive on the beach, with Laura holding a hula hoop up in exactly the perfect spot (we used a tape measure to be sure). Certain conditions were not the same as they would be on stage at The Joyce: I was running on sand, there was no glass, and the frame was being held, not hanging. I surmised that this rehearsal set-up would be good enough to establish my aim-and-dive distance.

Then, on the last dive of the morning before we left for the airport, I broke my foot. I must have power-punched on a rock or something. At the time, I thought I only had a heel bruise. It hurt like the dickens: not really pain but an interesting, rather foreign sensation that I felt with each step I took. I didn't know it was broken until several days later.

I got to The Joyce with hardly enough time to get dressed and onto the stage. I stood upstage center, staring at the frame with my heart pounding out of my chest. I have never not been terrified before a performance, but this was much worse than usual. The lights went out, except for on the glass onstage. I crouched down and time went by, a little too much time. I was waiting to be ready. Then I knew I wasn't going to be ready, so I shot downstage with every corpuscle of metal blood gristle muscle bones sinews pushing, thrashing out of me. I let out a blood-curdling scream as I launched my body and my mind at that glass, punching so hard the glass flew into the first three rows of the audience. I landed, at least two feet downstage of the frame. It was stock still, with a big hole in it. Glass was everywhere. It only lasted two seconds.

"Breakthru," ES diving through glass, 1997.

NOTES

IN THE BEGINNING

1. Audi, Robert, ed. *The Cambridge Dictionary of Philosophy* (Cambridge: Cambridge University Press, 1999), 399.
2. Guerlac, Susanne. *Thinking in Time: An Introduction to Henri Bergson* (Ithaca, NY: Cornell University Press, 2006), 18.

BODY

1. Albrecht, Ernest. *The New American Circus* (New York: Henry Holt, 1989), 317.

SPACE

1. Le Corbusier. *The Modulor* (Basel, Switzerland: Birkhauser Publisher of Architecture, 2000), 65.
2. Parr, Adrian, ed. *The Deleuze Dictionary* (New York: Columbia University Press, 2005), 257.
3. Kant, Immanuel. *Critique of Pure Reason* (Cambridge: Cambridge University Press, 1997), 157.
4. Bennett, Jonathan. *Kant's Analytic* (Cambridge: Cambridge University Press, 1966), 30.
5. Serra, Richard. *Weight and Measure 1992* (London: Tate Gallery, 1992), 25.
6. Cole, K.C. *The Universe in a Teacup: The Mathematics of Truth and Beauty* (Orlando, FL: Harcourt Brace & Company, 1998), 54.
7. Deleuze, Gilles. *Bergsonism* (New York: Zone Books, 1997), 49.
8. Kwinter, Sanford. *Rem Koolhaas: conversations with students* (New York: Princeton Architectural Press, 1996), 84-85.
9. Le Corbusier. *The Modulor*, 65.
10. Crouch, Tom D. *First Flight: The Wright Brothers and the Invention of the Airplane* (Washington DC: National Park Service, US Department of the Interior, 2002), 75.

TIME

1. Crouch, *First Flight*, 64.
2. Kaku, Michio. *Hyperspace: A Scientific Odyssey Through Parallel Universes, Time Warps, and the 10th Dimension* (New York: Anchor Books, 1994), 232.
3. Bergson, Henri. *Matter and Memory* (New York: Zone Books, 1988), 139.
4. Greene, Brian. *The Elegant Universe* (New York: W.W. Norton, 1999), 72.
5. Ibid., 139.
6. Smith, Norman Kemp. *Commentary to "Kant's Critique of Pure Reason"* (Highland, NJ: Humanities Press International, 1996), 138–39.
7. Ibid., 138.
8. Davies, Paul. *About Time: Einstein's Unfinished Revolution* (New York: Simon and Schuster, 1995), 80.
9. Ewing, A.C. *A Short Commentary on "Kant's Critique of Pure Reason"* (Chicago: University of Chicago Press, 1967), 178.
10. Greene, Brian. *The Fabric of the Cosmos: Space, Time, and the Texture of Reality* (New York: Vintage Books, 2004), 77.
11. Klein, Stefan. *The Secret Pulse of Time: Making Sense of Life's Scarcest Commodity* (New York: Marlowe and Company, 2007), 72.
12. Kant, *Critique of Pure Reason*, 179.
13. Sherover, Charles M., ed. *The Human Experience of Time: The Development of Its Philosophic Meaning* (Evanston, IL: Northwestern University Press, 1975), 173.

MOTION

1. Mulhall, Stephen. *Routledge Philosophy Guidebook to Heidegger and "Being and Time,"* 2nd ed. (New York: Routledge, 1996), 176–77.
2. Bergson, Henri. *Time and Free Will: An Essay On The Immediate Data of Consciousness* (Mineola, NY: Dover Publications, 2001), 110.
3. Braun, Marta. *Picturing Time: The Work of Etienne-Jules Marey (1830–1904)* (Chicago: The University of Chicago Press, 1992), 281.
4. Pais, Abraham. *Subtle is the Lord: The Science and the Life of Albert Einstein* (Oxford: Oxford University Press, 2005), 179.

Harry Houdini.
"Straightjacket escape."

APPENDIX A

ACTION HEROES

From the libretto written by Laura Flanders for the STREB show "Action Heroes—The Story of Transgressive, Outlawed, and Untidy Action in America," 2000.

EVEL KNIEVEL

Notwithstanding a fractured nose, jaw, skull, back, hip, knee, pelvis, shin, and sternum, broken arms, ankles, wrists, toes, clavicles, and every rib, motorcycle daredevil Evel Knievel says he's done everything he ever dreamed of. In all the years spanning his death-defying leaps (including jumping over fifty stacked cars and thirteen Mack trucks) and crashes, he never ducked a promise to the public. Reflecting on his life, the showman has said, "I'd do it all the same, except I'd go faster on a few jumps." PHOTO: GETTY IMAGES.

CANNONBALL RICHARDS

Richards had a routine: to catch a cannonball in his gut. Flat feet anchored in the fairground dirt, he'd plant himself before the cannon's mouth and let a lead ball shoot into his belly. The sideshow crowd would holler, and think him primitive and absurd. But to Richards, his was a feat of mass-momentum: flying. From Atlantic City to Chicago, he'd be knocked with force into the prototype trampoline behind him, then bow to the crowd, unsmiling. They'd laugh, but he knew better. He was the famous one: Cannonball Richards, lateral acrobat.

STREB: Action Heroes

SHIPWRECK KELLY

Alvin Anthony Kelly was a sailor, a boxer, and a steel-girder walker. Building Manhattan's skyscrapers taught him to have no fear of heights. On a standard-issue flagpole, Kelly would perch on a platform no bigger than a fancy dinner plate and consume colas, donuts, or burgers—whatever his sponsors paid him to promote. With his thumbs jammed in two bore-holes to wake him if he was leaning, Kelly catnapped in "cloudland." In Madison Square Garden in 1929, he stood for twenty-two days on a pole above a dance marathon. While the couples below forced themselves to keep moving, Kelly stood still and stole the show.

PHOTO. REPRINTED WITH PERMISSION FROM THE *NEW YORK DAILY NEWS*.

HARRY HOUDINI

Master of the manacle, the box, the breath, and every eye, Harry Houdini arrived in the US from Hungary in 1878 to become the world's most revered escape artist and magician. Breaking out of a presidential assassin's jail cell? Wriggling out of a straightjacket while dangling from his ankles from a tall building? Escaping a submerged packing case filled with six hundred pounds of iron weights in the New

York Bay in under three minutes? No problem. For all your foils and fears and fakeries, Harry Houdini, we salute you: supreme showman of the small space.

PHOTO: REPRINTED WITH PERMISSION FROM THE SIDNEY H. RADNER COLLECTION, THE HISTORY MUSEUM AT THE CASTLE, APPLETON, WI.

LARRY WALTERS

Larry dreamed of flying in his own homemade machine. In 1982, at the age of thirty-three, he attached forty-two weather balloons to a lawn chair, tethered the contraption to his Chevrolet, sat in the chair, untied the ropes, and rose. Not thirty feet, not forty, not one hundred, as he imagined. Above his girlfriend, his mother, and the family's suburban ranch house, Larry rose sixteen thousand feet over Los Angeles with not even a seat belt on his chair. A few miles out to sea, a startled commuter pilot saw Larry float past his cockpit. An alerted rescue helicopter at last towed Larry home. But Larry was already saved. To fly was all he wanted. After Larry landed, his arresting officer asked why he'd done it. He was curious, said Larry. Besides, "A man can't just sit around." PHOTO: AP/WORLD WIDE PHOTOS.

ANNIE EDSON TAYLOR

Circus man Bobby Leach did it later but it took six months to heal his injuries. Charles Stephens was a lion tamer but it killed him all the same. George the Greek was a philosopher—he died doing it with his turtle. People have tried in oil tanks, bouncing balls, plastic caskets filled with Styrofoam; they've traveled with oxygen tanks and walkie talkies, but of the ten who've crossed the Niagara Falls and lived, Annie Edson Taylor was the first. In 1901, Taylor, a widowed schoolteacher, did it fully dressed in a petticoat and wooden barrel, plain.

PHOTO: REPRINTED WITH PERMISSION FROM THE NIAGARA FALLS (ONTARIO) PUBLIC LIBRARY.

LYNNE COX

The marathon swimmer's body is the one machine she's got. From the air, sharks, and ice water, skin is the only separator. In 1987, thirty-year-old Lynne Cox became the first person to swim across the Bering Straits, from Alaska to Siberia. Wearing a Speedo swimsuit, the water ten degrees above freezing, and the swimmer's horizon at her nose, Cox completed her journey in two hours and six minutes.

PHOTO: REPRINTED WITH PERMISSION FROM THE ALEXANDER TURNBULL LIBRARY AND THE EVENING POST COLLECTION.

161

PHILIPPE PETIT

Men and women of the high wire walk a cable whose center is named the soul. Their stage is half an inch wide, in the sky. "Private poetry in public space," Philippe Petit has called it. Petit spent six years engineering a walk between New York's World Trade Towers. Six years to walk one hundred and fifty feet, on an illicit wire, one hundred and four stories above the street. For years, the window washers preserved Petit's signature on the outside of the South Tower where he left it. Petit once said, "When a man begins to tremble for his life, he begins to lose it." PHOTO: POLARIS IMAGES.

TEHCHING HSIEH

Thirty-one million, five hundred and thirty six thousand consecutive seconds with one other person at the end of an eight-foot rope—Tehching Hsieh tied himself to fellow performance artist Linda Montano for a year. Their mission: never to separate and never to touch. Sharing neither a common language nor the same taste for food, they shared every room, every movement, every instant and that rope. On the fourth of July 1984, after 364 days, a friend cut their

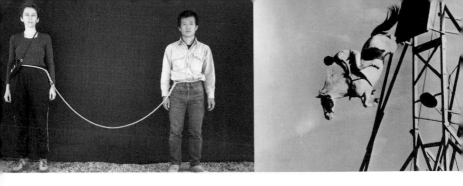

nylon bond with a knife. Before the rope, Hsieh spent a year in a cage, forbidding himself to talk, read, write, watch television, or listen to radio. Another year was spent living outside, never leaving Manhattan and never going indoors. For a brief time a painter, Hsieh concluded early on, "Action on the page is too smooth."

SONORA CARVER

In 1920, sharpshooter Doc Carver placed an ad in the newspaper for a girl who could swim, dive, and travel. Twenty-year-old Sonora Carver signed up. For nineteen years, Sonora and her horse would leap from a platform sixty feet above the ground into a twelve-foot tank, even after the force of the water on one jump left her blind. The blindness wasn't such a big deal, said her sister, "The horse was in charge." Besides, it expanded one's sense of the possible, said onlookers—that size, that speed, that splash.

APPENDIX B

Q&A

Anna Deavere Smith
& Elizabeth Streb

What follows is a segment of the thirty-minute Q&A with Anna Deavere Smith and Elizabeth Streb

ADS: I thought it would be good to see what ends up happening if it's like a half hour, and that's all it is—finite.

ES: Yes—

ADS: When I observe your work, even though there are obviously optical illusions in there somewhere that we can't see—there is something very serious about, you know, either you can fall backwards or you can't. It seems as profound this time.

ES: Movement.

ADS: Yeah. Your—in your case, movement seems as profound as time.

ES: Yes.

ADS: And so I wanted to talk to you about time.

ES: Movement is probably not as fundamental as time. It's basic. For instance, you can take movement and break it down into more parts than just movement. Requires space, requires body, if you're talking about physical movement, and it requires time. So in that sense, it could still be profound, but not as fundamental.

ADS: But man constructed time.

ES: Yes. There is—there is purportedly no arrow of time, no vast future. It's just now. And so, it's a convenience so the trains run on time, et cetera. The practical issues. But so far, no one's been able to come up with a proper, clear scientific definition of time that works in all circumstances. Probably, you know, even if Bergson is talking about movement, he will say there is no movement, it's just thousands of positions, and that's what creates the temporal structure because to get it from the first one to the thousandth one, it takes time and it's not in time.

ADS: What's the temple structure? What does that mean, the temple structure?

ES: The *temporal* structure. Well—

ADS: Oh, temporal.

ES: Temporal. Yes, temporal structure.

ADS: Uh huh, okay.

ES: Meaning—I mean, that's a crazy thing. Things pass through time, but what is it? So, if we're going to describe—if I'm going to look at you moving, but I don't want to just focus on your body, I want to look at the actual act you are performing, which is invisible, you know, it hasn't happened yet, until you've done it, and then once you've done it, it's gone. You're on to the next thing. But that also hasn't occurred yet. And so, that's why if you focus—if you're body-centric, time goes unnoticed, the action of the time that it takes to perform that action.

ADS: Really?

ES: Yeah. So what we're trying to—

ADS: Tell me what you mean by body-centric.

ES: Well, when people watch people moving, like in ballet, you go to a normal dance concert let's say, not a STREB show, but a normal dance concert—they are very focused on the body. They are looking at the positions the body makes. In fact, ballet spends most of its time on that, and then the rest of the time gets spent on getting the muscles to the right part of the skeleton, and also on being able to perform their—their vocabularies perfectly to the classical music they are using. I mean, the most—the most purely classical idea of ballet is with classical music.

So they'll spend time fitting the body into those timing systems that are encased in classical music. But people don't look into the body. They are not naming the action. They're naming the moves. It's just the—also, if you look at the nomenclature, you realize, oh, glissade, petite allegro, grand allegro tour jeté. Those are moves the body is doing.

So they're not naming the temporal rhythmic structures of the invisible action that the body is performing. Do you know what I mean?

ADS: Kind of.

ES: I mean, why we believe movement has to be extreme is so that you'll stop noticing the body, and then it's like—it's like it's abusive, really—rather than showing somebody something, you're letting something happen.

ADS: Okay.

ES: And I think that's a profound distinction between undoing something. Well, you can't do something if the conditions are so extreme, you're not able to perform them. In fact, it slips into a zone that things are happening to you.

ADS: Right. Right.

ES: And you're trying to survive, and clearly, you need all that skill. But it's not that you're doing something.

ADS: Well, they are doing something, but I think where we meet you is something could happen.

ES: Something could happen.

ADS: A [steel bar] comes at them, but they avoid the bar.

ES: Right. Right. They avoid it at the last second because of where the drama in motion is, not too much margin, because you want the causality also. If we're going to say that the true—if you were going to try and think about a temporal structure that's purely physical, then you would have to contend with causality, and causality is a series of events. Once you—but the first cause, the first act, is—I can't um, theorize about that cause, that's where my theory falls apart. It has to start somewhere? And that's artificial. Once it starts the second move can't happen without the first, the third move can't happen without the second, et cetera. And so let's say a cement block's coming like this? And the dancer's doing something *in* that space that the block will soon be in but *just* leaves as the block passes. If the dancer left when the block wasn't even near them, there would be no subject happening. So I'm saying that—yes it's about avoiding getting hit but it's more about trying to construct a moment that is dramatic and physical.

ADS: Hm hmm.

ES: So, I am saying that, yes, it's about avoiding getting hit, but it's more about trying to construct the moment that is dramatic and physical.

ADS: Hmm. What's the difference between you and the circus other than (say) midgets, clowns, and elephants?

ES: Well, the difference between me and the circus—and I really learned this by performing with Cirque du Soleil at their twentieth anniversary. They invited us to perform up in Montreal. And I tried to analyze—and I think what's the difference? The audience doesn't— didn't notice. I thought the audience would boo us off the stage because a circus act that . . .

ADS: Hm hmm.

ES: But the audience didn't notice. And I came to the conclusion that it was a grammatical difference.

ADS: Hmm.

ES: That it was syntactical—that our actions are—the constructions of our actions are longer, the sentences are—more formed. It's not—and there is a paragraph. It may not be a chapter like a story ballet would be, like *Sleeping Beauty*. I don't do books. And I don't believe in those types of stories. This is not about— literalness. But it's about can you construct a physical moment and have it be essential. And I think the physical moment in circus is prepositions and conjunctions.

ADS: So, it's shorter?

ES: Way shorter, and they are—that's why they—

ADS: It's acts.

ES: It's acts. It's tricks.

ADS: Tricks?

ES: Oh—constant. Like, I keep thinking, oh, I can feel the audience. We just performed in Boston last week, and I was thinking, [whispering] the audience wants to clap right now but we just keep going.

ADS: Right.

ES: What the circus does is—

ADS: Right.

ES: —stop constantly—

ADS: So that you can clap.

ES: Yeah.

ADS: Wow.

ES: And, so, I am still struggling with what—whether—is that how you perform movement? Does the circus with its enormous medieval history—ancient history rather—they know how to present it to the audience.

ADS: Wow.

ES: Stop. Stop. Stop. Constantly. We just keep on going, and I have a feeling it's a formal obnoxious exhibition of privilege.

ADS: Yours.

ES: Yes, that we keep going. I haven't gotten there yet.

ADS: But that has to do with time too.

ES: This is delicious wine, Anna.

ADS: I'm glad you like it, 'cause I know you like red wine.

ES: It's so, so sweet of you.

ADS: Oh . . .

ES: I'm telling you the truth.

ADS: So—

ES: Tricks. Tricks. Tricks. Tricks.

ADS: Tricks. Tricks. Tricks.

ES: Um. Well, people would look into what we do and see a flip—and say, well, that—yeah, some people think that STREB does tricks. We're doing virtuosic, what the old postmoderns, the Judson Church era people, like Yvonne Rainer—

ADS: Ahhhhhh.

ES: And all those people. Although I mean Yvonne would say it right out, she—"No to virtuosity." I don't know what she thinks about it now, but her *No Manifesto* claimed that no training, no virtuosity, no—I mean, I should check that. But definitely no virtuosity. No exhibition of that. It was all pedestrian.

ADS: That's what she said?

ES: Yes, at the time, 1962?

ADS: That was her goal?

ES: Well, they just did task-oriented movements. But that—it was like John Cage's silence of four minutes and thirty-three seconds where he sat at the piano and didn't play. . . . But I always was sad because to me—um, I remember her walking by me when I first came to New York. I was in my twenties, and she had already left dance. And I said, "I know you don't know me but I am sad every day that you left dance." And she said, "I didn't leave dance." And I said, "Oh, okay." But I think the deal was that tricks, that virtuosity—we are virtuosic, and I believe that we try to *gain* virtuosity for the—you know, to help *contain* our effort to survive *severe* situations and conditions that we construct within our, um, template of our show—of our spectacle. And I do that not to present the skill, but to use it to avoid—disaster.

ADS: Ummmm hmm. Right!

ES: To move that fast, you cannot be a lug and only moving medium speed.

ADS: Right.

ES: And get out of the way of a whizzing bullet. I mean, you cannot do it. You cannot fall from thirty feet in two-thirds of a second and figure out how to get your body in the right spot—before you land. You know, you'll die. So, I believe our interpretation of virtuosity is different and it's not about executing tricks.

ADS: Right.

ES: That we know how to execute it. Although, you're looking at: we do flips, we do a lot of those gymnastic moves that are, if you would rather just say formally they are the big muscle groups. Snapping is fast as the petit allegro that the ballet people use a technique for moving their feet that fast. That's just transferred to the *big* muscles, the glutes and the quads and *snapping* them in half a second. And when you do that, your entire hundred and seventy pound body goes into the air, or hundred and sixty pound—

ADS: You are probably going to write about what I'm going to ask you in your book, and it's probably not a very good question: Why do you cherish being in contact with disaster? Why is that so critical to who you are and your work?

ES: Well, I believe it is where the true human movement lies. I do believe that's where it is, in physical terms. And if I was going to have the—a different discipline to express what I think is true in the world and it wasn't movement, I would probably make different choices.

ADS: Like what?

ES: Like—

ADS: To still be in contact with disaster?

ES: I probably wouldn't need to do that, but I don't think—it really goes back to, you know, as everything does, to very formal inquiries in each of our fields, and for me, in movement, I've noticed that you cannot ignore the quality or the act of perception in the witnesses who are not moving. You know, so you ask this very simple question: "I wonder how people perceive movement?" You know, and as I mentioned that I think that the disaster—the failure of flight or the crushing, the ultimate crushing and disintegration of the human body—is really what movement is about.

ADS: Say that again.

ES: The crushing or the disintegration of the human body is ultimately the final act of movement in the world that we know, and so it's not that I am trying to be sadistic or masochistic. I just really believe that that is the language of movement that I can get the audience to notice. And then I think it has to do, ultimately, with the rhythms that that provides. And if you're not moving radically through space, and dealing with it really—actually not just right side up on your feet—then you're—there are no rhythms that are noticeable because you're punctuating the air. And you're punctuating the ground with actual aural information, and if it's an intense enough punctuation, you're spatially creating moments that can be construed into a rhythm. And if I don't do it in an extreme manner which would lead to the disaster zone, it's not noticeable. People are just going to keep looking at my body.

ADS: Hmm.

ES: Their reaction—

ADS: But we do look at your dancer's bodies.

ES: In the off moments, maybe.

ADS: No, constantly.

ES: You think you do?

ADS: For sure.

ES: When they're falling and everything?

ADS: We're not just—I mean definitely. Definitely. Definitely. Definitely 100 percent and you pick good-looking people.

ES: I think they're gorgeous.

ADS: Why do you pick good-looking people?

ES: They really—they happen to be beautiful, but I think what's really interesting, if you looked at them in their regular clothes and not watching them move the way they move but pick them for how they move, the manic, maniacal, crazy people are the ones that want in there. I mean, they still have to be careful enough to be able to go on stage when we need them to. But I feel that they're—I pick them for how they have this particular relationship with movement once they start generating through space, their bodies.

ADS: But they're good-looking people, and, you know, when they came here to see the show and they were backstage, I—you know, it didn't—I didn't register that they were your people. I mean, there were a group of people who'd come backstage and I saw them. You—look—at—them. They are *attractive* people. In a room full of people, my eye went right to them. And even though they may not be on the cover of *GQ*, they are attractive. Your eye goes there.

ES: Beauty.

ADS: So, I think you *do* look at them.

ES: Well, do you think though, that—I mean, there's levels of noticement. So you *do* look at them. But is it the first thing you see, or is that something that trails off of what they do?

ADS: I think you do look at them, and people—I'm sure people must look at their calves . . . Do any of them get letters or anything like that?

ES: You know, I don't know. I sort of stay out of that. They do. I see letters coming. I don't know who they're from.

ADS: Do they have people hanging around afterwards to meet them—

ES: Yeah.

ADS: See. 'Cause they're looking at them.

ES: They're looking at them. Well, I guess I don't really focus on that. I do like beautiful people. I think that—I mean, in the end, it's a performance art? I don't

know—it's all relative, who's beautiful and who's attractive.

ADS: Because you said you don't look at the dancers. That's how I took off.

ES: Yeah, I know and I guess I'm making—I mean that— I mean my goal is that there only be action on the stage.

ADS: You see, that's—

ES: Until—

ADS: I feel that's a little bit sadistic.

ES: You do?

ADS: Yeah. I met this director of Samuel Beckett's plays whose idea was to use Beckett to knock the meaning out of the words.

ES: Yeah. That is so beautiful.

ADS: It's like to take—

ES: Yes.

ADS: *To knock—the meaning out.*

ES: That's beautiful. I would imagine that Beckett at a certain point, I mean, when he came along in the theater era, at the time when he did, you're knocking the meaning out of words because they could become so cliché-ridden.

ADS: Hm hmm.

ES: You're just trying to reimbue those words with the actual meaning that this is what the word I intend, and this is what that word will mean. Cleansed of all the past meanings.

ADS: Mmm.

ES: And if you could imagine people like—I mean, if you

watch dance concerts, those dancers, they look like they spend a lot of their time looking in the mirror and they do.

ADS: A lot of time.

ES: And they do. And that is what has to be pervasive. And so I guess I'm thinking as they knock the—not knock the personality out of that person because they have a lot of personality they have time to exhibit on stage. But not in the middle of the inaction of a real move, whatever that would mean.

ADS: Did you—when did you decide to take the mirror out of dance?

ES: I've never used it. Right when I first started training in my teens. I couldn't look in the mirror. I was like thinking—I just, you know you think idiotic, idiot savant thoughts. I just thought, why do they have a mirror in here? You can't move and look, move and look.

ADS: But you studied dance for a long time. You didn't use —you didn't look in the mirror? How did you get your positions right?

ES: Positions were not my—I had teachers. I would, like, cross my eyes when I looked in the mirror. I didn't really—I wasn't interested in my positions. I was interested in being able to *do* things.

ADS: Okay. So, now I'm going to ask a psychological question that you're probably—you *should* hate. I would hate it if somebody asked me. I would think, what a really boring—person. So, do you think that your flirtation, do you think that your flirtation with disaster—I'm kind of fishing for the questions so forgive me is probably not quite right—do you think that your flirtation with disaster has anything to do with the fact that you were almost without a mother?

ES: You mean my birth mother? I didn't know my birth mother.

ADS: You didn't know your birth mother. You could have grown up in an orphanage.

ES: Yeah.

ADS: And somebody else came in and—a beautiful person, this mother you have told me about. She came in and she took care of you. I mean, do you think that your flirtation or do you think you are liberated to flirt with disaster because you had this very profound thing happen when you were—

ES: Two.

ADS: —a baby.

ES: The first two years.

ADS: Yeah.

ES: Well, I mean, I guess I find that sentimental. You know, and I guess if my first impulse, after an experience like that, being an orphan, would have been sentimental, then, I think I would have exhibited sentimentality.

ADS: At *two*?

ES: Well, I think that—yeah, you'd feel sorry for yourself. I mean, you wouldn't—at two—remember that you did it. But you would look back and create an iconography, kind of this storyboard of how y'know, moments in your life were sad, and you would construct your personality around those sadnesses, the things that happened—

ADS: And you didn't do that?

ES: Well, I don't believe I am one of those people that care—

ADS: But I mean at two, you may not have even known you didn't have a mother.

ES: Of course. You think no one has a mother. You think everyone is adopted. I thought everyone was adopted until, you know, I found out that that's not usual to be adopted. But I think the attachment and worrying about yourself . . . I think, to be a real true movement, maverick maniac, which is the only kind of movement—I just so happened to be interested in—you really can't be into a self-preservation mode. Not for yourself, not for other people. And that type of flirting—well if, I mean your question, the root of your question is more complex than that. Do I think that's why I like to go to the—go to death's door, peer through, and escape and feel cool that I escaped? Well, what is that? I don't know. What that is. I'm sure it's not altogether [almost inaudible] healthy, but I've created a world in my movement exploration where it's my language. It's part of my language. And I haven't really talked a lot to psychiatrists.

ADS: Well, I don't really think it's necessarily the domain of psychiatry.

ES: You don't think?

ADS: No. I mean, I think it's unfortunate that we medicalize and authenticate explorations of our mythology by taking it to a doctor.

ES: You do? You think that—

ADS: I think that's weird.

ES: You do?

ADS: Yeah. I think there are many other places that we could meet in terms of looking at the story that we were given by chance.

ES: Right.

ADS: By chance we were given a certain story—that we don't have anything to do with.

ES: Yeah. Nothing.

ADS: You know, you were in that orphanage, right?

ES: Yeah.

ADS: So we don't know—we don't—and so—I don't think it has to be a pathology. That's why I don't think it belongs to a psychiatrist. I think it belongs in another area of storytelling, and mythology—a myth, a great myth. The great myth of *you.* So it's curious because I remember from our other interview the story of you carrying the water up the hill—

ES: That's in the book—

ADS: —so that your father, your father, there is some place for him in the story that has to do with stamina, and I'll show you, right?

ES: Right.

ADS: So, I wonder about your mother in your myth, and if there is any place where anything about those primal years have to do with your *profound* love affair with disaster.

ES: Yeah. Uhhh. Maybe getting—this would become, I mean, if I was going to make it less than what I really think it is, I've used it to do what I am doing now. But

I—you know, when you're a kid, I was trying to get attention away from my sister who was a wild child. And maybe it was just a, you know, pathetic, effort to get some extra attention. I don't really think so—

ADS: Doing disastrous things—

ES: Burning barns down and—

ADS: You wrote about that in the book, burning down the barn?

ES: But these are just little snippets because my editor wanted me to do that. But I think that—I always felt really together. I mean, I excelled in studying. I really liked to study. I mean, I don't feel that I was—

ADS: If you burned the barn down, how come you didn't become a juvenile delinquent?

ES: Well, I, you know. They were gonna—it was my age. I didn't have to go. I was supposed to go to juvenile court. Very true. It was arson.

ADS: How old were you?

ES: I think I was twelve.

ADS: You dress a little bit like an old-fashioned 50s juvenile delinquent.

ES: [She laughs heartily] I don't think anyone has ever given me a better compliment.

ADS: I mean it as one.

ES: You do?

ADS: Yeah.

ES: A 50s juvenile delinquent. A JD.

ADS: Do you think of yourself like a—do you think you're the part of a juvenile delinquent?

ES: In the dance world you mean?

ADS: In the world. Do you think of yourself that way at all? Do you embody—do you take on that, you know, fraction of a myth that we were—but do you embrace that notion of the juvenile delinquent, even as you're basically a goody-goody?

ES: Well, I think that let's say I'm sitting down and I'm going to say to myself, okay, what move must I do next? I'll think of—I'll try to think of—it's very hard to think of a move until it happens to you. But I'll try and think of something that would be so outrageous that a body would never be able to do it. No one's ever seen that move before et cetera et cetera et cetera. But I don't think of myself anymore since I'm not a practitioner of embodying . . .

END OF THIRTY MINUTES

ACKNOWLEDGMENTS

Laura Flanders has channeled air beneath my wings for close to two decades. She has shared with me a more clairvoyant view of the world as seen from the eagle's eye-view. She is my deep love, my passion, and my life changer. Laura took an initial draft of my masters thesis called "The Real Move Manifesto" and excavated my antigrammatical jumble of thousands of words; she sprinkled magic dust onto my five page sentences, and culled sensibility, meaning, and a certain graceful beauty out of an undecipherable landscape of clouded thoughts. Laura was responsible for proposing this manuscript to Amy Scholder, my editor at the Feminist Press, and had the first idea of this project as a book.

Catharine Stimpson pointed toward heaven's gate and dared me to reach it. She invited me to New York University as the Dean's Distinguished Scholar in 1998, and after a full ten years suggested it might be time for me to graduate. I received my masters degree in 2008, awarded from the John W. Draper Interdisciplinary Masters Program in Humanities and Social Thought, part of the Graduate School of Arts and Science at NYU.

Robin Nagel, the director of the Draper Program, was my navigator—steadfast, kind, and inventive. She helped me at every turn and in every way. Allen Mincer, my math/physics tutor for the first five years, took me ardently through all three of the Amsco textbooks, which were necessary preparation for me to enter the precalculus and calculus I university level studies. Taking these classes took another few years. I want to thank Professor Gilad Lerman, who was my mathematics teacher. He spoke philosophically, clairvoyantly, and profoundly, about the measurements of areas under curves. Professor Thomas de Zengotita helped clarify my sense of the philosophers and was a brilliant interpreter of their thoughts and oddly complex and esoteric intentions in regard to space, time, motion, and being. This was most notably true in regard to the ideas found in Heidegger, Wittgenstein, and Kant. Andre Lepecki agreed to be my thesis advisor and my teacher for his course in performance studies called, Deleuze and Guattari. With cryptic wit and patience he showed and guided, without telling, the essence of non-arborial systems of knowledge.

Thanks to my sister, Lori Chambers, who led the way into beautiful wildness and pure freedom of spirit, I followed.

My artist-soul-partner and best friend is Danita Geltner. We met in 1977 as young artists, and for the past thirty-three years we have examined together why all life is all art in the end. Danita sees colors when the sun is not out, and eeks out the human aspects of life on earth in a poetic and deeply empathetic embrace. She reminds me what being a practicing artist is really all about.

Amy Scholder was the person who said Yes. I had wanted to write these ideas down and spread them around in order to start a dialogue with the action-interested world. She made this book possible. The memoir sections of the book were her idea; the order, the organization, including deciphering what were ideas that belonged in time and which were those meant to be in space, even though we both knew you can't technically separate them. It's space-time, and time-space all the way down. Thank you. I deeply thank the rest of the phenomenal team at the Feminist Press, especially Jeanann Pannasch, for her grace and beautiful writing. Thanks also to Drew Stevens, for his perfect book design. And the tireless intrepid interns at the FP, Ayana Smith and Lauren Raheja. Thanks to Gloria Jacobs, the executive director of the FP, for seeing this through. They all tacitly agreed to shepherd me through the rapids of making a thesis into a book. Thank you, FP.

I want to thank Barry Cipra, my mathematics consultant for the last number of years. And Anna Deavere Smith, a staggoringly original artist, whom I revere. She has single-handedly birthed an entire movement of new languages and methods, and morphed the aural into a new category of actual physical rhythms. She has irrevocably added to the lexicon of theater and is a visionary leader in the invention and delivery of live-time events. Anna captures the heart of the human condition to tear-filled and joy-imbued results. Thank you, Peggy Phelan, a vivid raconteur who plays hardball with my practitioner ideas. With her disagreements, she forces harsher diligence from me. Thank you Trisha Brown, Philippe Petit, Kathy O'Donnell, and Mikhail Baryshikov.

I want to thank Kim Cullen at the STREB Lab for Action Mechanics (S.L.A.M.) who holds, imagines, and controls the container for our exploits with movement. For their guidance and effervescent support, thank you Cynthia Mayeda, a cultural leader who is infinitely kind and harsh when required; and Ben Cameron, who has sculpted theories and analyses about the criticality of culture and its engines in the US. Both have outlined in the air, land, and sea, invisible and magical structures for artists to work and play in.

Thank you to Susan Meyers and Cathy Einhorn, who have been our development team at STREB and S.L.A.M. for the past fifteen years, and have worked untold and mighty miracles. Deep thanks to our keeper of the flame and of the books, Henry Liles. My gratitude to STREB's highest and mightiest angels to date, Sage and John Cowles. With the widest and most elegant wingspan, a blind faith, and a love in the power of movement, they bought our first box truss and made the first three years of S.L.A.M. possible.

Thanks to my stunning and brave board of directors, with Andrea Woodner at the helm—a perspicacious, wise, and Socratic leader, I'd follow her off any cliff; with Paula Gifford McKenzie, a veteran STREB dancer of ten years, who helped to cull the moves we now do with shocking and stellar aplomb. To Suzanne Shaker, the beautiful and gentle giant of possibility; to Harry Mizrahi, our Board Treasurer, who advised and demanded our legitimacy; to Robert Reitzfeld, who invented STREB's logo and gorgeous, brilliant monikers establishing how the world sees us graphically; to Craig Tooman, for lobbies, roofs, and Big Love; to Ellen Salpeter, who shapes not-for-profit reality, shedding light on possibility; to Helen Marden, who provides gorgeous and original places to be in the world and on the walls; and to Cheryl Batzer, Stephanie Blackwood, Sheron Davis, Laura Michaels, and John Charles Thomas.

And for various reasons, without the presence of the following people I wouldn't have a story to write: George Loening, Doug Steiner, Kate Levin, Susan Chin, Kathy Hughes, Ed Jones, Craig Dykers, Snøhetta, Manuel Igrejius, Carl Vollmer, Margaret Ratner Kunstler, Mitchell Kurtz, Rena Shagan, Paul Wolf, John Denham, Andy Lance, and Sarah Fowlkes.

For all the dancers, current and past, who have added to the language of our physical knowledge, and who have left behind traces of their spirits, ideas, and moves, and who still reside in the walls of our hearts and minds and lay embedded in the concrete, steel, and swirling air of our invention rooms. They include Sarah Donnelly, Cassandre Joseph, Chris Lee, Daniel Rysak, Samantha Jakus, Jackie Carlson, Fabio Tavares, Leonardo Giron Torres, Kevin Lindsay, Joshua Martinez, Ami Ipapo, Christine Chen, DeeAnn Nelson, Terry Dean Bartlett, Christopher Batenhorst, Aaron Henderson, Jonah Spear, Chantal Deeble, Weena Pauly, Nikita Maxwell, Eli McAfee, Lisa Dalton, Sheila Carreras Brandson, Brian Brooks, Hope Clark, Brandon O'Dell, Matthew Stromberg, Christine McQuade, Michael Schwartz, Boris Willis, Diann Sichell, Joseph Arias, Daniel MacIntosh, Nancy Alfaro, Jane Setteducatto, Henry Beer, Peter LaRose, Jorge Collazo, Gary Lutes, Brian Levy, Katrina Birchfield, John Landes, Paula Gifford, Mark Robinson, Soldana Rivera, Ned Malouf, Adolpho Pati, Christina Knight, Liam Clancy, Guadaloupe Martinez, Alma Langley, and Jason Jaworski.

INDEX

Page numbers in italics indicate photographs.
C indicates color photograph pages.

Abramovic, Marina, 45
absolute space, 81, 112
absolution of the seam, *xix–xx*
acceleration, 38, 53, 90, 131, 141
action
    audience perception of,
      71–73, *72*
    conscious framing of, 73
    defining meaning in, 20–21
    nexus for, 132
    spatial perception and, 73–75
    stories told by, 34
    transformation of, 42–43, 45
    unpredictable, 42
action heroes, *xvii*, 42
"Action Heroes" performance, *58*
action karaoke, 17
action lexicon, *xviii*, 11, 21,
    25–27, 37–38, 119, 134, 167
Action Machines
    Artificial Gravity rotating
      floor, 86–92, *86, 116,*
      C1–C3, C6–C7
    body as action machine,
      101–102

    defining space and, 81, 83
    design of, 83–84
    "Gauntlet" pendulum,
      122–123, 124–125
    as musical instruments, 83
    spinning I–beam, 92–93, *93*
    SuperPosition, 93–95, *94*
    turning body on turning
      wheel, *144*
actions
    action rhythms, 134
    action specialists, 40–41,
      45–47
    lexicon for, 21, 25, 27, 134
    performance as event, 45–47
    response to extreme actions,
      54
    as subject, 57
acts of will, 48–51
adagios, 5, 34
Adams, Douglas, 42, 127
aesthetics of movement, 42
aging and death, 51
airborne dance, 34, 37, 75, 77
"Airlines" performance, *C1–C3*

analog information storage, 109

angle of viewing, 26, 60, 65, 74, 75, 90

angular momentum, 88–89

animal instincts, 132–133

anti-intuitive movements, 79–80, *79*

a priori nature of time, 23, 105, 107–108

archetypes of movement and action, 21, 23, 147

arena, 59–63

"around the world" flips, 145

"arrow of time," 104, 110, 166

"art act," 10

"Artificial Gravity" performance, 86–92, *86*, *116*, *C1–C3*, *C6–C7*

aspect ratios, 60–63

audience
    body-centric focus of, 57, 59, 166–167
    disbelief of, 125
    experience of, 25, 106, 117, 119, 142, 149, 169–170, 173–174
    eye views of, 65, *66*, *67*, 68, *69*
    physical reaction of, 85
    rules of conduct for, 16–17
    spatial perception and, 71–73, *72*
    un-habitual space and, 63–65, *64*

Babb, Roger, 31

back falls, 79–80, *79*

ballet training
    dancing to music and, 99, 167
    hunks of action in, 99
    looking in mirror and, 98, 177
    opinions of, 31, 34–35
    techniques, 145–146

Ballou, Bill, 83

"ball" position of PopAction, 130

Banach-Tarski theorem, 53

barn burning, 5–6, *6*

Baryshnikov, Mikhail, 45

Beaumont, Cyril, 145

beauty, *x*, *xi*, 174–176

Beckett, Samuel, 176

being, 98–99, 103–104

Bennett, Jonathan, 71

Bergson, Henri
    on language and thinking in time, 24–25
    on making images, 113
    on movement, 137, 139, 166
    on present moment, 103, 104
    on real duration, 117

Bessie Awards, *79*

"BiLevel" performance, *100*

"BlazeAway" performance, *xiii–xiv*, *xxii*, 27–29, *28*

body
    "againstness" of Merce Cunningham, 43
    being used up at moment of death, 51
    body-mind connection, 142–143
    dancers' bodies, *xi*, 174–176
    effect of dance on, 33–34
    habits of use, 42

body, *continued*
  orientation of, 37, 65, 76, 79
  smearing, 95
  strength and training of,
      40–41, 120–121
  turning body on turning
      wheel, *144*
  un-habitual space and, 63–65,
      64
  as vessel for action specialists,
      21, 46–47, 101–102
"bottom" concept, 37
"Bounce" performance, *44*
Brain Café, (Babb), 31
brain response to danger, 39
bravery, 49–51
break-dancers, 84
"Breakthru" real move, 149–151,
    152–153
Brooklyn Borough President's
    Office, 16
Brown, Tricia, 43, 45
Bruckner, Ira, 55–56
Brunelleschi, Filippo, 73
bull riding, 98–99
Burden, Chris, 45
Burke, Edmund, *xviii–xix*
burning barn, 5–6, *6*
burning body, "BlazeAway"
    performance, *xiii–xiv, xxii,*
    27–29, *28*
Byer, Diana, 31, 145–146

Cage, John, 3, 33, 45, 171
"call and response" system, 28
carefulness of modern dance,
    38–39

Carson, Heather, 119
Carver, Sonora, 163, *163*
"Casino Pool" photograph, *72*
Casselli, Michael, 83, C14
causality, 63, 103, 132, 146, 168
Cecchetti ballet, 145–146
cement blocks, "Gauntlet" perfor-
    mance, *122–123*, 124–125
change and movement, 107
Chaplin, Charlie, 45
Charlie and Kelly's restaurant,
    9, *10*
Chomsky, Noam, 137
choreography
  audience perception of space
      and, 71–73, *72*
  "Breakthru" real move,
      149–151, *152–153*
  dance design and
      development, 80, 83,
      124–125, *135*
  early interest in, 9, 11, 33,
      97–98, 139–140
  eye view design and, 65, *66,*
      67, 68, *69*
  grace and motion and,
      xviii–xix, 136
  noticing action and, 57, 133
  sensory gaps and, 112
  staging design, 60, 61–63, 117,
      119
  vertical air space and, 43
  wasted space and, 68, 140
circular motion
  "Artificial Gravity" stage
      design and, 62, 86, *86,* 89,
      92

"PolarWander" performance, C4–C5

"Revolution" performance, 82, 85, C14

SuperPosition machine and, C12

circus performers
circular arena, 61
duration of actions and, 169–170
as inspiration, 45
Moscow Circus, 50–51
training of, 40

Cirque du Soleil, 169

Clark, Hope, 41

class structure in dance, 35, 46–48

Clay, Roger, 110

clichés, 43, 78, 134, 176

"clump" position of PopAction, 130

Cole, K.C., 11

comfort zone, 39, 63, 76, 134

constructed uproar, 89–92

content
accomplishing real moves and, 90–91
of movement, 21, 57
noticing actions and, 133–134
past actions as oral history, 47
rhythm and real action, 137
ten-second dance and, 115

cooking career, 8–11, 10

Corvino, Alfredo, 31

counterweighted motion, 94, 94, C9, C12–C13

Cox, Lynne, 45, 161, 161

Craske, Margaret, 31, 34–35, 145–146

Crowder, Phil, 83

Cunningham, Merce, 31, 33, 42–43

dance
critiques of performances, 25–26
as falling down, 31
gender behavior in, 34–35, 42
historical tasks of movement in, 26
music as enemy of, 113–114, 119, 132
need to experience in time, 23
training in, 31–35, 32, 98, 102, 176–177
vocabulary of STREB technique, xviii, 21, 25, 27, 134, 167
see also choreography

Dance Theater Workshop, 33

danger, 20, 37, 39–41, 48, 75, 134

D'Apolito, Justin, 83

Davies, Paul, 110

Death and Life of Great American Cities (Jacobs), 17

Deep Survival (Gonzales), 39

dégagé ballet exercise, 146

The Deleuze Dictionary (Parr), 68

Deleuze, Gilles, 68, 81

de Moroda, Friderica Derra, 145

design of dances, see choreography

De Zengotita, Thomas, 104

digital information, 109, 116
distilled movement meaning, 137
diving through glass, 149–151, *152–153*
doing and rhythm, 113
drawings, 80, 83, *135*
"Drop" bungee cord performance, *58*
duration of things, 81, 117
Dykers, Craig, 45

Easy Rider (film), 55
Edgerton, Harold Eugene, 139
Edwards, Mary, 31
eel memory, 3–4, *4*
efficiency of movement, 121–122
Einstein, Albert, 83, 103–104, 110
elitism, 35, 46–47
Ellison Park Hill, 128, 129–130
emergency actions, 45–47
equipment, *see* Action Machines
equiprimordial elements, 107
Espana, Ivan and Noe, 41, 45, 83, 94, C12
Euclid, 104, 112, 143
events, *see* extreme physical actions
Ewing, A.C., 112
exhaustion of meaning, 68
experimental places, 16–17
extreme action specialists, 46, 111, 116
extreme physical actions
desire for, 29, 33–35, 85, 101–102
existential nature of, 131–132

experience of, 16–17, 23, 35
performances, 85
psychic effects of, 49–51
eye views of audience, 65, *66*, *67*, 68, *69*

falling
back falls, 79–80, *79*
catching falling box, 97–98
as dancing, 31
free falling, *36*, 50–51
relative motion and, 76, 141
"RunUpWalls" performance, *C8–C9*
skiing and, 130, 131
see also flying
fall line, 131
Fanger, Iris, 114
Farber, Viola, 31
fast-twitch muscles, 39
fear, 38–39, 41
Fibonacci spiral, 87, *87*
fight or flight response, 39–40
film and television aspect ratios, 61
Finch, June, 31
fire in dance performance, *xiii–xiv*, *xxii*, 27–29, *28*
fire escapes, 11
fixed seating in theaters, 17
Flanders, Laura, *xxii*, 27–29, *28*, 149–150, 157
Flanders marina, 3–4
flux, 104
flying
desire to fly, 35, 97
free falling, *36*, 50–51

landing and, 37–38, 53
learning how to fly, 75–80,
    77, 79
missing the ground epigram,
    127
STREB dance company and,
    17
"Wild Blue Yonder"
    performance, C10–C11
The Flying Cranes, 45
"Fly" performance, 20, 64
forces
    Action Machines and, 81, 82,
        83, 84–85, 85
    Artificial Gravity machine
        and, 88–92
    dance and, 38
    final force at moment of
        death, 51
    invisible, 120–125, 122–123
    learning to fly and, 75–80,
        77, 79
foreign sensation, xi, 38–39,
    119–120, 151
Fraleigh, Condia, 31
free falling, 36, 50–51
Fried, Michael, xx

Galdamez, Karla, 142
galloping horse, 139
Gambino, Jimmy, 8
"Gauntlet" performance,
    122–123, 124–125, C16
"Gauntlet x 3" performance, 118
Gehrig, Cynthia, 149
Geltner, Danita, 27, 184
gender and dance, 34–35, 42

Gettier, Edmund, 24
Giglio, Santo, 31
glass "Breakthru" real move,
    149–151, 152–153
Glassman, Bill, 31
golden mean, 87, 87
Gonzales, Laurence, 39
grace and motion, xviii–xix, 136
grammar of movement, xviii–xix,
    137
gravity
    Artificial gravity machine and,
        89–90
    attaining un-habitual space
        and, 145–147
    going fast and, 119–120
    landing and, 37–38, 53
    stillness and, 76
Greene, Brian, 104, 112, 143
Grossman, Nancy, 45
Guerlac, Suzanne, 24

Hadid, Zaha, 45
hamster wheel, human-sized, 82,
    85, C14
happenings, 104
Hardware Junkies, 83
harmonic measurement of
    space, 61–63, 62
"Headstand" photograph, 20
heel drives, 77–78, 77
hegemony of ground and floor,
    17, 64, 75, 134
Heidegger, Martin, 103, 107,
    130–131
Henkin, Leon, 111
hidden dimensions, 84, 143

hidden memories, 21, 23
Honda 350 motorcycle, 7–8, *7*,
    53–55, 101
horizon line, 73–74
Houdini, Harry, *22*, 45, 50, *156*,
    159–160, *160*
Hsieh, Tehching, 162–163, *163*
human motion, 41–43, 45, 57
Humphrey, Doris, 31
Humphrey-Weidman dance
    technique, 31
hunks of action, 99, 101–102,
    113–114
Hutton, Lauren, *x, xi–xii*

impacts, 17, 20, 37–38
inner approach to training, 40–41
investigation of space, 78–80
invisible forces, 120–125,
    122–123
isometrics, 90

Jacobs, Jane, 17
James ("block guy"), 8
Jazz at Lincoln Center, 124, C16
Jeffers, Jan, *4*
Jenkins, Margaret (Margy), *32*,
    33
Joseph, Cassandre, 94
The Joyce Theater, 149
jumping, 77–78, *77*
juvenile delinquents, 181–182

Kaku, Michio, 104
Kant, Immanuel, 23, 70, 103–104,
    105–112, 115–117
Keaton, Buster, 45

Kelly, Alvin Anthony
    "Shipwreck," 159, *159*
Kitty Hawk "Wild Blue Yonder"
    performance, *C10–C11*
Knievel, Evel, 45, 158, *158*
knowing and knowledge, 23–24

"Lake Sunapee Dive, New Hamp-
    shire" photograph, *69*
Landau, Max, 13–14
landing and dance, 17, 37–38
language of action and
    movement, *xviii,* 11, 21,
    25–27, 37–38, 119, 134, 167
leaping versus flying, 35, 37
Le Corbusier, 61, *62*, 63, 87
Leibniz, Gottfried, 106
Let Me Down Easy (play), *xii*
lexicon of action and movement,
    xviii, 11, 21, 25–27, 37–38,
    119, 134, 167
lightness in ballet, 34, 37
Limón, José, 31
"Little Ease" performance, *19*
live-time events, 26, 59–60, 116,
    119, 185
"LookUp" performance, 65, *66*,
    67, 68
Lorenz, Jocelyn, 31

machines, *see* Action Machines
Madison Square Garden, 50, 159
making-present, 131
*A Manual of Theory and Practice
    of Classical Theatrical
    Dancing,* 145
Marden, Brice, *x*

Marden, Helen, *x,* 186
Marey, Étienne-Jules, 139
Margaret Jenkins Dance Studio, *32,* 56
Matta-Clark, Gordon, 45
meaning
    accomplishing real moves and, 90–91
    of movement, 21, 57
    noticing actions and, 133–134
    observers of movement and, 137
    past actions as oral history, 47
memories, 3–5, *4,* 21, 23
meta-movements, 76, 89
methods
    dance teachers and training, 31, 98
    stage design and, 88
    STREB choreography and, 63, 80, 133–134
models, *x, xi*
modern dance, 7, 38–39, 47, 146
moments, 109
momentum, 90
mortality, 51
Moscow Circus, 50 51
mother, 127–128, 178–180
motion
    archetypes of, 21, 23
    fight or flight and, 39–40, 132–136
    grace and, 136
    human, 41–43, 45, 57
    speed and, 128–132
    see also movement

motorcycle, Honda 350, 7–8, *7,* 53–55, 101
movement
    anti-intuitive, 79–80, *79*
    concepts of, 21, 25, 47, 137, 139
    early memories of, 97–98, 99, 101–102
    effects of, 23, 33–34, 47
    episodic nature of, 115–117
    staying alive and, 57–58
    stillness and, 76, 106, 124, 141–142
    syntax of, 136–140, *138*
    time as refuge of, 117, 119
    unnecessary, 68, 140
    see also real moves
"moviecal" movement show, 142
Muhammad Ali, 45
muscle groups, 39, 41–42
Museum of Contemporary Art, Los Angeles, *66*
Musgrave, Story, 59
music
    Action Machines as, 83
    as enemy of dance, 113–114, 119, 132
    movement as stepchild of, 26–27
Muybridge, Eadweard, 106, 139–140

Nagrin, Daniel, 31, 33
naming process, 119, 167
Nevelson, Louise, *ix*
The New American Circus (Albrecht), 40

195

Newman, Barnett, 73
Newman, Susannah, 33
Newton, Isaac, 104, 112, 134, 143
New York City Council, 15–16
New York City Department of
    Cultural Affairs, 14, 16
New York City Loft Law, 13–14
New York City Mayor's office, 16
Niagara Falls, 48, *49*, 161
nomenclature for actions, *xviii*,
    21, 25–27, 37–38, 119, 134,
    167
non-predictive outcomes, 46
now
    categories of, 130–131
    duration of present tense,
        106, 114–115
    real moves and, 25
    STREB actions and, 115–117,
        116, 118

Old Dutch Mustard Company, 14
"open source" rule for audience
    behavior, 16–17
opera and symphony stage
    design, 60
oral history, 47
"Orbit" performance, C14, *C15*
outside space, 68, *69*

Paige (girlfriend), 11
pain, *see* foreign sensation
Panetta, Janet, 31
parallax view, 74–75
Pauline, Mark, 45
pendulums, 122–123, *122–123*
perception of movement, 70–80

perspective, eye views and,
    64–65, *64, 66, 67,* 68, *69*
Petit, Philippe, 45, 91, *162,* 612
Phelan, Peggy, *xvii*
photography, 140
physical clichés, 78–79
physical experience
    of audience, 65, 74–75
    existential nature of, 131
    pain and, 39
    STREB methodology and,
        133–134
physicality
    achieving real moves, 40
    body's potential for, 48–51
    desire for, 29, 33–35, 85,
        101–102
    memories of, 3–5
    willingness to embrace, 47–48
physical phenomena, 20, 89
physical skills, 45–47
physical world, 56–57, 84
physics, 109, 142–143
place and space in dance, 43, 45
Plexiglass wall in "Ricochet"
    performance, *xx–xxi*, C14,
    C15
Plyshenko, Irma, 31
"PolarWander" piece, *93,* C4–C5
Pollock, Jackson, *xxi*
PopAction movement technique,
    xvii, 41–42, 103, 130
possibility concept of future, 131
potentiality of space, 68
practice, 51
predictability, 46–47
present tense, 106, 114–117

proscenium, 60, 70–71
psychic effects of extreme
    actions, 49–51
public moments, 3–4
public space, 13–14
purity, 23–24

Rainer, Yvonne, 171
Randall, Lisa, 84, 104
rats, 9, 12
raw space, 12–14
reality, 105–112
real moves
    audience experience of,
      25–26, 73
    "Breakthru" real move,
      149–151, *152–153*
    concepts of movement, 21,
      23, 25, 47, 137, 139
    danger and, 39–41, 48–51,
      98–99, 141–142, 167–169,
      172–174
    definitions of real, 21, 23–26
    flying and, 75–80, *79*
    as holy grail, 20, 41
    intellectual consideration of,
      24–26
    investigation of space and,
      78–80
    recognition and creation of,
      33–34, 40–41, 68, 141–142
    removal of transitions from,
      xix, 42, 129
    rhythm and, 113–115, 137,
      173–174
    STREB dancers and, 40–41,
      75–80, *77*, *79*

    timing and pacing of, 105–
      112, 119–125, *122–123*
    un-habitual space and, 63–65,
      89, 132
    see also Action Machines
real time, 16–17, 105–112
rehearsal, 51
relationships, 11, 13–14
relative motion, 76
relativity theory, 110
restaurant career, 8–11, *10*
"Revolution" performance, *82*,
    85, *C14*
rhythm
    Action Machines and, 95, 145
    as archetype of motion, 21,
      137
    ballet and, 145–146
    innate, 6–7
    nomenclature for, 134
    pure locomotion and, 133
    spatial rhythmics, 42–43,
      173–174
    time and, 113–115, 119, 167
Richards, Cannonball, 158, *158*
"Ricochet" performance, C14,
    C15
risks, 54–56, 120
rules of audience conduct, 16–17
running radius, 88
"RunUpWalls" performance,
    C8–C9

Sample, Cathy, 54–55
San Francisco, 54–56
San Francisco Ballet School, 56
scarification, 45, 47–48

sentimentality, 43, 49–51, 178
Serra, Richard, 45, 73–74
SHAM dance piece, 33
sheetrock memory, 4–5
signifiers of time, 81, 122–124,
    166
skeletons, 41
skiing, 128–130, *129*
S.L.A.M. (STREB Lab for Action
    Mechanics)
    xii–xiii, 14, *15*, 16, *36*
    see also STREB dance
    company
Slayton, Jeff, 31
"small things," 17
Smith, Anna Deaveare, *ix,*
    165–182
Smith, Norman Kemp, 107
Snøhetta, 45
snowshoes, *128*
sound barrier, 48
space
    action machines and, 81, 83
    audience perceptions of,
        71–73, *72*
    Banach-Tarski theorem, 53
    design and structure of real
        moves and, 21, 59–63, 68,
        79–80
    investigation of, 78–79
    motorcycle road trip and,
        53–56
    noticing action and, 57, 133
    perspective and eye view
        design, 65, *66, 67*, 68
    un-habitual space, 63–65,
        64, 84

vacant space above dancers,
    61–62
    see also real moves
"Spacehold" performance, 80
spatial curiosity, 40
spatial flexibility, 65, *66, 67*, 68
spatial perception, 73–75
spatial rhythm, 42–43
spatial separation, 71–73, *72*
speed
    leaving space and, 110–111, *111*
    reluctance of humans to go
        fast, 119–120
    skiing and, 128–130, 131–132
spinning I-beam Action Machine,
    92–93, *93*
"Squirm" dance piece, *22*
stage design, 60, 61–63
"Stand" dance concept, *135*
Stanford, Leland, 140
State University of New York at
    Brockport, 6–7, 31, 33
"Stepping off the edge"
    performance, *1*
stillness, 76, 106, 124, 141–142
stomach smear, 95
stories, 43, 179–180
Strasser, Rose, 6–7
Streb, Carolyn Elliot Gale,
    127–128, 178–180
STREB dance company
    birth of, 17, *18, 19*, 20–21, *20*
    body investigation and, 38–39
    densifying air with actions,
        116–117
    learning to fly and, 75–80,
        77, 79

methodology, *xix*, 40–42,
    129, 133–136, 145–147,
    149–150
PopAction and, 41–42
S.L.A.M. (STREB Lab for
    Action Mechanics), *xii–xiii,*
    14, *15*, 16, *36*
on time and space, 93, 132
see also Action Machines;
    choreography; real moves
Streb, Leonard, 4–5, 12–13,
    54, 101–102, 180
supercollider experiments,
    110
SuperPosition Action
    Machine, 93–95, *94,*
    C12–C13
superstring theory, 84, 143
Survival Research
    Laboratories, 45
Suzie (dog), *128*
Swimmer, Eddy, 35

tachyons, 110
tactual-kinaesthetics, 71
"Target" performance, *18*
Taylor, Annie Edson, 45, 161
temporal curiosity, 40
temporal structure, 166
tenant rights, 13–14
téndu ballet exercise, 146
ten-second dances, 115–117
terminal velocity, 130
theaters, 16, 20
theater tickets, 17
theatrical moments, 77, 142
theatrical space, 68

theoretical physics, 84, 110,
    143
350 Honda, 7–8, *7,* 53–55, 101
The Three Stooges, 45
thrownness concept, 131
tickets, 17
tightrope walking, 39, 91, *162*
time
    audience perception of moves
        and, 106
    as container for movement,
        106
    as element of real moves, 21,
        92–93, *93*
    as fundamental, 165
    invisible forces and, 120–125,
        122, 123
    now and present tense,
        103–104
    real time, 105–112
    rhythm and, 113–115
    signifiers of, 81, 122–124, 166
    speed and choreography,
        119–120
    ten-second dances, 115–117
    Trisha Brown's choreography
        and, 43
    see also now
training
    cooking career and, 9
    in dance, 31–35, *32*, 98, 102,
        176–177
    performances as events,
        45–47
    STREB methodology and,
        xix, 40–42, 129, 133–136,
        145–147, 149–150

transfer method of locomotion, 41

transformation of movement, 33–34, 98–99

transgressive actions, 54

transitions, *xix,* 42, 129

trapeze artist training, 40

Treadwell, Tom, 12–13

tricks, *xi,* 170–172

"trueness," 24

true rhythm of action, 21, 23, 133

true space and flight, 17

true timing-length, 121–122

truth, 23–24, 41

Tseih, Tehching, 45

turbulence, 46, 89–92, 134, 135, *C6*

un-habitual space
  Action Machines and, 81, 83–84, 89
  audience perceptions and, 63–65, *64*, 78
  challenges of attaining, 145–147
  learning to fly and, 75–80, 76, *77, 79*
  The Universe in a Teacup (Cole), 77

un-Lincoln Center, 16

unpredictable action, 42, 46–51

"up" concept, 37

urban barn, 16

vanishing point, 73

Verdery, Aaron, 83

vertical space
  flying and, 37
  horizon line and, 73, 74
  Merce Cunningham and, 42–43
  "RunUpWalls" performance, *C8–C9*
  un-habitual space and, 63–65, *64*, 78

virtuosity, 171–172

vocabulary of STREB technique, *xviii,* 11, 21, 25–27, 37–38, 119, 134, 167

Vollmer, Carl, 14

Wagenfuhrer, Martha E., 48, *49*

"the walk of the drunken people," 90–91

Wallenda Family, 39–40

"Wall" performance, *138*

Walters, Larry, 160

Wheeler, John, 105–106

"Wild Blue Yonder" performance, *C10–C11*

"wrecking" a place, 16

Wright Brothers, 81, 92, 101

Yeager, Chuck, 48

MacArthur Fellow **ELIZABETH STREB** founded STREB Extreme Action Company in 1985, which performs internationally in theaters, museums, and town squares. She established S.L.A.M. (STREB Lab for Action Mechanics) in 2003, a factory space in Williamsburg, Brooklyn, which produces a cottage industry of extreme action performances and invites everyday people to wonder about movement, gravity, and flight.

Actor, playwright, and author **ANNA DEAVERE SMITH** performed her latest play *Let Me Down Easy* off Broadway and appears on Showtime's *Nurse Jackie*.

PEGGY PHELAN is the Ann O'Day Maples Chair in the Arts and professor of drama and English at Stanford University. She is the author of *Unmarked: The Politics of Performance* and *Mourning Sex: Performing Public Memories*, among other works.

LAURA FLANDERS is the host of GRITtv, the news and culture discussion program seen online at GRITtv.org and on satellite, public, and cable television. She is the author of *Blue Grit: True Democrats Take Back Politics from the Politicians* and *Bushwomen: Tales of a Cynical Species*.

The Feminist Press is an independent nonprofit literary publisher that promotes freedom of expression and social justice. We publish exciting writing by women and men who share an activist spirit and a belief in choice and equality. Founded in 1970, we began by rescuing "lost" works by writers such as Zora Neale Hurston and Charlotte Perkins Gilman, and established our publishing program with books by American writers of diverse racial and class backgrounds. Since then we have also been bringing works from around the world to North American readers. We seek out innovative, often surprising books that tell a different story.

See our complete list of books on at **feministpress.org**, and join the Friends of FP to receive all our books at a great discount.

THE FEMINIST PRESS
AT THE CITY UNIVERSITY OF NEW YORK
FEMINISTPRESS.ORG